The Campus History Series

BENEDICTINE
MILITARY SCHOOL
IN SAVANNAH

The Campus History Series

BENEDICTINE MILITARY SCHOOL IN SAVANNAH

Robert A. Ciucevich

ARCADIA
PUBLISHING

Published by Arcadia Publishing
Charleston, South Carolina

Printed in the United States of America

Library of Congress Control Number: 2020937203

For all general information, please contact Arcadia Publishing:
Telephone 843-853-2070
Fax 843-853-0044
E-mail sales@arcadiapublishing.com
For customer service and orders:
Toll-Free 1-888-313-2665

Visit us on the Internet at www.arcadiapublishing.com

This book is dedicated to my father, John Edward Ciucevich Jr., class of 1960,
who inspired me to write about the people and places that mean the most to me;
to John Cavuoto, Edward M. "Toby" Buttimer, and Terry E. Brewer,
classmates, friends, and brothers; to the generations of Benedictine monks,
who have dedicated their lives to forming Savannah's young men in
body, mind, and soul; and especially, to Br. Tim Brown, OSB,
for none of this would have been possible without his early support.

(Courtesy of Betty Ann Ciucevich.)

CONTENTS

ACKNOWLEDGMENTS

Like any history, the writing of this book was informed by the works of the past—the research and accounts of both professional and amateur historians—as well as the recollections of those who lived the history recounted in these pages. The framework of much of this history is their contribution, for which I give my thanks and appreciation. In the same way that their work proved vital in the writing of this account, I hope someday that this book will provide a stable foundation for other historians to build on as well.

Of the many works that informed the writing of this book, I am particularly indebted to Jerome Oetgen's *The Origins of the Benedictine Order in Georgia*, which provided the lion's share of source material for chapters one and two; Gary Wray McDonogh's *Black and Catholic in Savannah, Georgia*, which provided the basis for the sections of chapters one, two, and three that deal with the establishment of St. Benedict's and Sacred Heart Parishes; and Fr. Paschal Baumstein's *My Lord Belmont: A Biography of Leo Haid*, which provided the basis for chapters three and four, particularly the sections dealing with the establishment of Sacred Heart Priory and Benedictine College.

Several people and organizations were instrumental in making this book possible. I would especially like to thank the monks of Benedictine Priory, who granted me unfettered access to the priory archives; Katy Lockhard, director of the Diocese of Savannah Archives & Records Management Office; Luciana Spracher, director of the City of Savannah Research Library and Municipal Archives; Simon Donahue, Belmont Abbey Archives; and Fr. Andrew Campbell, archivist of St. Vincent Archabbey.

I would also like to thank Arcadia Publishing, especially my editor Caroline Anderson, and Mike Dillon of the Benedictine Alumni Association. Mike, who graduated from Benedictine in 1968, was a wealth of information.

And of course, I would like to thank my wife, Kara; my mother, Betty Ann, who answered many of my questions; and the rest of my family for their patience and support.

Unless otherwise noted, all images appear courtesy of the Benedictine Priory Archives.

INTRODUCTION

I wear the ring. I wear the ring and I return often to the city . . .
to study the history of my becoming a man.

—*The Lords of Discipline* by Pat Conroy

These, of course, are the opening words of Pat Conroy's book *The Lords of Discipline*, his ode to the military academy. The city he is writing about is Charleston, South Carolina, and the school he is referring to is the fictional "Carolina Military Institute," a thinly veiled reference to his alma mater, the Citadel. Yet, any graduate of a military school could easily evoke his own experience and school in reading these lines. As Conroy writes in the author's notes:

> This novel is about the idea of the military school and the various forms it has taken around the country. I interviewed men from West Point, Annapolis, the Air Force Academy, Virginia Military Institute, the Citadel, and dozens of military high schools around the South in preparation for writing the novel. There is a sameness to all of these schools; yet each is unique and has its own fiercely protected identity.

This is certainly true of Benedictine Military School in Savannah, Georgia. The uniqueness of the school cannot be denied; anyone familiar with Benedictine, also known as "BC," would agree. Yet it does, as Conroy states, share a "sameness" with other military schools. It has a well-organized and disciplined Corps of Cadets, and it has its own decades-long traditions, beloved teachers, and legendary military instructors. Unlike other military schools, BC was founded and operated by monks of the Benedictine Order. It is this distinction that sets Benedictine apart, not just from other military high schools, but from other secondary schools as well.

The unique blend of military order and monastic discipline employed at Benedictine is not a new concept; during the 19th and early 20th centuries, other Catholic high schools around the country had robust military programs, but few have been as successful in its execution. While the military aspects at these schools faded and were eventually terminated, the military program at BC accelerated and endured. Today, Benedictine remains one of the oldest and finest military high schools in the nation.

Benedictine was founded by monks of Belmont Abbey, North Carolina, in 1902. Abbot Leo Haid established the military program at Benedictine College because he felt that it would provide "the environment that would best encourage the proper enrichment of youth." He believed that "a military program would develop the boy physically and mentally, and create habits of promptitude and order, foster self-reliance, and inculcate in the student, as part of his nature, manly ideas of obedience, loyalty, discipline, and courtesy." In adopting the prestigious military academy model for Benedictine College, the Savannah monks created an ordered and structured environment that promoted a disciplined approach to studies and virtue, an approach that complemented their own monastic lifestyle and aided in their overall goal of forming young men in "body, mind, and soul." It is this combination of military order and discipline and the Benedictine ideals of obedience, moderation, stewardship, and community, among others, that make Benedictine a unique place.

The very nature of Benedictine foundations, like the military school, further amplifies its singularity. Benedictine communities are independent and self-governing; it is this autonomy that allows each Benedictine community to form its own identity. Through the vow of stability—a vow unique to the Benedictine Order—Benedictines make a commitment to a particular community for life, a particular geographic place, and, in seeking to be the best stewards of God's gift of place, draw upon the culture, history, and traditions of the locality in which they, the monastic community, find themselves. As a result, the hundreds of Benedictines who have lived and taught here have come to identify themselves with this Savannah community, and we, in turn, have identified with them. At Benedictine, earning a diploma does not signify an end, but instead a beginning, a lifelong commitment to the values and ideals that the school and its monastic community represent. Generations of Benedictine alumni can attest to this truth because they "wear the ring."

I began writing this book in an attempt to provide a history of Benedictine Military School and to create a record of its traditions and rich heritage. I felt that the only way to accomplish this was to also trace the history of the Benedictine Order in Georgia, as it would be impossible to separate one from the other. There are several accounts of the early origins of the Benedictines that I hoped to combine with other not-so-well-known accounts of the priory's and school's past. *Benedictine Military School in Savannah* chronicles, in images and text, nearly 150 years of Benedictine presence in the Savannah area. The book explores the heritage and traditions of this Catholic, all-boy's military high school as well as the shared legacy of the monks of Belmont Abbey who founded the school, and the monks of St. Vincent Archabbey in Latrobe, Pennsylvania, who operate the school today.

St. Benedict wrote his rule for cenobites around 540 A.D. as a guide for monks living within a community ruled by an abbot. Although never intending to found an order, Benedictine monasticism spread rapidly across Europe, becoming the dominant monastic observance in Western Christendom by 800 A.D.

The Rule of St. Benedict consists of two parts: a spiritual component, which instructs the monk how to live a life centered on Christ, and an administrative component, which instructs how to run a monastery efficiently. The spirit of the rule is summed up in the mottoes of the Benedictine Order: *pax* (meaning "peace") and the traditional *ora et labora* ("pray and work"), as well as the order's guiding principle, which is "that in all things God may be glorified."

The Benedictine vow of stability provides a keen sense of responsibility to the environment that has guided Benedictines for centuries to embrace the *genius loci*, or "the spirit of the place," in establishing their monastic foundations throughout the Western world.

Benedictine monasticism spread to the United States in the 19th century when Boniface Wimmer, a Bavarian monk of St. Michael Abbey in Metten, Germany, established St. Vincent Priory, the first Benedictine monastery in America, at Latrobe, Pennsylvania, in 1846. According to esteemed Benedictine historian and Wimmer biographer Jerome Oetgen, Wimmer hoped to transplant to the New World the "ancient Benedictine Order from Europe" where Benedictines

> had founded centers of spirituality, learning, and culture . . . and for nearly
> thirteen centuries, had made unparalleled contributions not just to the

dissemination but, at times, to the very survival of Western civilization. During the early Middle Ages, Benedictine communities, and the schools attached to them, had kept the light of faith and learning alive as barbarian tribes descended upon Europe, destroying the fabric of the old Roman civilization.

Education had always played an important role in the Benedictine tradition, and since the earliest times, schools were attached to the monasteries where there developed a "heritage of humane and liberal learning centered on such Benedictine values as stability, community, hospitality, and moderation," according to Oetgen.

Wimmer implemented the monastery-school model of his predecessors at St. Vincent, which was elevated by the pope to the rank of abbey in 1855, and at each of the five dependent monasteries—or daughter houses—he founded throughout America, all of which eventually became independent abbeys.

Unlike other religious orders, Benedictine communities are independent and self-governing, as prescribed in the Rule of St. Benedict. It is this autonomy that allows each community to develop its own identity. Stability, the vow to live in one community for life, has a great influence on the spiritual life of the monk. A Benedictine's site of stability, the monastery where he professed vows, becomes sacred ground, his spiritual home. In the words of Br. Benet Veten, a monk of Blue Sky Monastery in South Dakota, "stability often puts us where God wants us to be."

Due to the missionary nature of the order, Benedictine abbeys establish daughter houses within the regions they are located, making it necessary for some of the monks within the community to live away from the motherhouse, their site of stability. Architecturally, daughter houses often reflect the heritage of the founding abbey while also blending in characteristics indigenous to the area in which it is located. Because daughter houses are founded with the expectation that they will one day become independent and rise to the rank of abbey, it is important for each monastic foundation, architecturally and spiritually, to have and develop its own identity and to become one with its environment.

STATUE OF ST. BENEDICT. This statue of St. Benedict originally stood on a pedestal in the monastic green between the quad and chapel. A similar statue now stands in the lobby of the academic building.

One

ISLE OF HOPE, GEORGIA

Ora et Labora *(Work and Pray)*

—St. Benedict of Nursia

In October 1866, forty-four Catholic bishops of the United States convened at the Second Plenary Council of Baltimore. Among the issues that were discussed was the obligation of the church to minister to the needs of the recently freed slaves. In April 1869, at the Tenth Provincial Council of Baltimore, the bishop of Savannah, Augustin Verot, took the lead among Southern bishops in proposing that the council require each bishop in the province to begin at once to build schools and churches for the black population. The proposal was adopted, and a decree was issued to that effect.

In 1870, the Diocese of Savannah was split, and Verot assumed responsibility for the newly established Diocese of St. Augustine. Verot was succeeded by Ignatius Persico, whose tenure as bishop of Savannah was cut short due to illness. In 1873, Persico was succeeded by Bishop William H. Gross, Congregatio Sanctissimi Redemptoris (CSsR), who immediately set about providing for the spiritual welfare of the 500,000 blacks, most of whom were freedmen, under his care. Gross applied to the abbot general of the Benedictine Cassinese Congregation of the Primitive Observance, the Right Reverend Raphael Tests, Order of St. Benedict (OSB), for missionaries to work among the diocese's black population.

Two Benedictine monks sent from France by Abbot Raphael arrived in Savannah on May 13, 1874. Soon after their arrival, Rev. Raphael Wissel, OSB, of Subiaco, and Rev. Gabriel Bergier, OSB, of Pierre-quis-Vire, established St. Benedict's Parish in the city, followed by a parish school. The early activity of the Benedictines attracted a great deal of interest among the local population, leading to a number of candidates to petition for admission to the Benedictine Order, both as clerics and as lay brothers.

In 1875, Father Gabriel purchased a small tract of land at the Isle of Hope, a peninsula nine miles south of Savannah, where he planned to establish a monastery and novitiate to house the growing community. The monks and several novices moved into the new building at Isle of Hope in the summer of 1876. It was the first Benedictine monastery established in the South.

ABRAHAM BEASLEY. This photograph of Abraham Beasley was taken in 1868. Beasley, one of 705 "free persons of color" living in Savannah in 1860, was a wealthy businessman who owned land, a restaurant, a saloon, a market, and a boardinghouse. While free blacks enjoyed certain rights and privileges that slaves did not, they were required to wear badges to indicate that they were indeed free. Beasley was a Catholic and attended Mass at the Cathedral of St. John the Baptist at a time when full segregation was not practiced, a condition that would change following the emancipation of slaves at the end of the Civil War. Despite his wealth, Beasley, as well as other Catholic blacks prior to the end of Reconstruction, was likely relegated to the rear of the church or the choir loft during services. (Courtesy of the Georgia Historical Society.)

BISHOP AUGUSTIN VEROT. Among his fellow Catholic prelates of the era, Augustin Verot, the third bishop of Savannah, was an early advocate of the spiritual and educational welfare of the freedmen under his care. By 1869 Verot had established, in the words of Jerome Oetgen, the "finest Negro school system of all the Southern dioceses" at a time when such an endeavor was not yet mandated by the church. (Courtesy of the Diocese of Savannah Archives & Records Management Office.)

ORIGINAL LOCATION OF ST. BENEDICT'S CHURCH. This 1888 Sanborn fire insurance map provides an illustration of the original St. Benedict's Church, built in 1874, which by this time had been converted for secular use as the Empire Hall. As the original edifice proved inadequate, the members of St. Benedict's Parish worshiped in temporary quarters for several years before another permanent sanctuary was constructed in 1889.

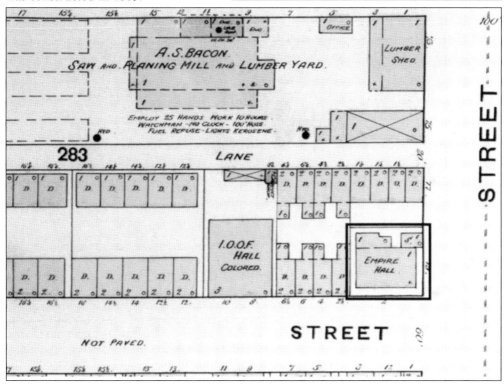

OUR LADY OF GOOD HOPE CHAPEL, ISLE OF HOPE, C. 1875. This photograph of the facade of the chapel dates from the early 20th century. An article from the February 15, 1875, edition of the *Savannah Morning News* detailed the dedication of the chapel:

> The 10:25 train on the Savannah, Skidaway and Seaboard Railroad carried down a large number of persons as participants in and witness of the ceremonies attendant of the new Catholic Church at Isle of Hope. Shortly after the arrival of the train a procession was formed at the residence of the Priest in charge of the Chapel, and marched to the edifice, which is quite a neat and comfortable building. . . . Major A. Bonaud, a resident of the Isle, donated the bell for the chapel, which was rung in the belfry on Saturday. Yesterday, as the procession moved off from the priest's house the bell was rung, the echoes reverberating through the woods. The ceremonies were quite interesting, Bishop Gross officiating, assisted by several of the Catholic clergy.

BR. PHILLIP CASSIDY, OSB. Br. Phillip Cassidy, pictured here, was the first Benedictine teacher in the South. In order to staff the parish school with teachers, Father Gabriel petitioned Abbot Boniface Wimmer of St. Vincent's Archabbey, and Brother Cassidy was sent from the monastery in Latrobe, Pennsylvania. The school opened in 1875 with an enrollment of 50 students, with Brother Cassidy serving as the first instructor. (Courtesy of St. Vincent Archabbey Archives.)

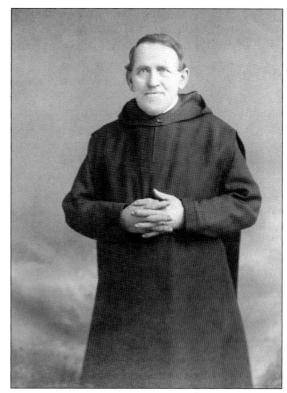

ISLE OF HOPE. This c. 1780 map, a portion of *Sketch of the northern frontiers of Georgia* by Sir Archibald Campbell, illustrates the distance between Savannah and the small, rural village of Isle of Hope, marked here as Parker's Ferry (lower left), where Father Gabriel established a small monastery. In the summer of 1876, the fledgling community of Benedictines moved into the new buildings, leaving Fr. Raphael Wissel in Savannah to run St. Benedict's Parish and Brother Cassidy to run the school. (Courtesy of the Library of Congress.)

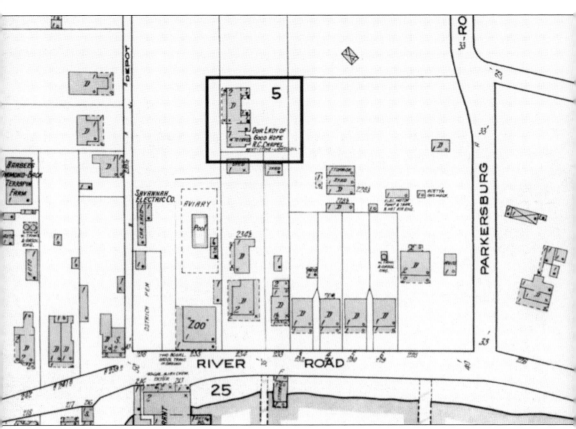

ISLE OF HOPE MONASTERY AND NOVITIATE. This 1916 Sanborn fire insurance map of Isle of Hope provides an illustration of the original monastery. Dr. Dupon, a Catholic resident of Isle of Hope, donated a small piece of land adjoining the monks' property. An existing building on the land was converted into a chapel, and as was traditional of Benedictine monastic architecture, a frame monastery was built off its side. During the fall of 1876, a yellow fever epidemic struck Savannah, and within a few months, the nascent community was decimated. Father Gabriel; a clerical novice, Frater Gregory Enright; and brotherhood postulant J. McDonald died. As support was lagging at the parish in Savannah, Father Raphael and the remnants of the community went to Oklahoma and joined the Benedictines of the Congregation of the Primitive Observance to work among the Native Americans.

OUR LADY OF GOOD HOPE CHAPEL, C. 1940. Here is a photograph of the chapel dating from around the 1940s; the two-story frame monastery building was no longer extant by this time. In 1908, the Right Reverend Bernard Murphy, OSB, a Savannah native, relayed his memories of the chapel and novitiate where he and his fellow novices professed simple vows to the Order of St. Benedict and where several members of the community perished during the yellow fever epidemic of 1876. When Murphy wrote a letter on November 18, 1908, recalling his time at Isle of Hope, he was serving as the third abbot of Sacred Heart Abbey in Pottawatomie County, Oklahoma: "Dear little chapel: How often have these hands scrubbed its floor, decorated its little altar and dusted the benches. I recall the good-hearted Dr. Dupon's gift to our struggling band. I alone remain of that once happy community, small in numbers, but joyful of heart." (Courtesy of the Diocese of Savannah Archives & Records Management Office.)

The good doctor had turned over the little place to the fathers who came to work for the Christian education of the colored people, many of whom I still recall by name. Anxious to have subjects among the youth o the city, a few Cathedral boys asked for admission. I was one among the chosen and with my dear boyhood friend, Joe Shea, received the habit of Holy Religion on the 6th of April, 1875.

Prayer and work became our daily task, and he, whom Our Lord took t Himself early in the priesthood, and the writer were inseparable, for ma years teaching, encouraging, etc., the colored children under our care. Others came to aid in the good work, both students and lay brothers. Several were colored, thus making an unique community, especially in a Southern state. Dark clouds were gathering, however, and early in the spring of 1876 we heard that the dreaded yellow fever had reached our beautiful Forest City. How faithfully all worked and with what heroic courage our priests and sisters faced the scourge. Alas! many of the de faces of my early youth went down to the cold grave and but few to see o shut their eyes in the sleep of death.

LETTER OF ABBOT BERNARD MURPHY, OSB, C. 1908. Bernard Murphy's letter, a section of which is pictured here, continues:

Among the little workers out at the Isle of Hope there was one who loved his fellow man deeply. Rev. Gabriel Berger, OSB, visited all classes and colors, bringing the consolations of holy religion to each even when his own health and community demanded his close faithful watchfulness. . . . The little home was to meet its sorrow, which proved to be so lethargic that the awakening comes but now. The writer, among others, felt the fever eating into his very bones. How fierce the burning, how short the trial for many. On the same bed with the writer lay one who within twenty-four hours was a corpse. Next evening there was another. Who was to bury the dead?—but a mere boy, what could one or two do to check our fear, our suffering? Only those who have felt may well describe the situation. A few weeks later and our beloved superior was carried off, after ministering faithfully to others. Our little band broken up, but the two named escaped to continue, out in the wild Indian Territory, their efforts for the red man.

Two

St. Benedict's Priory, Skidaway Island, Georgia

Forward, Always Forward

—Archabbot Boniface Wimmer, OSB

Following the departure of Fr. Raphael Wissel and a few members of the original community, Bishop Gross turned control of St. Benedict's Parish over to a diocesan priest, Fr. Fridon Eckert, and petitioned Abbot Boniface Wimmer of St. Vincent's Archabbey to assume control of the foundation at Isle of Hope and to establish a school for black children there. In March 1877, Fr. Oswald Moosemueller, OSB, and Fr. Maurice Kaeder, OSB, arrived in Savannah to take possession of the monastery at Isle of Hope. Finding the buildings in miserable condition and upon learning of the availability of a more suitable location on nearby Skidaway Island, Father Oswald accepted Bishop Gross's offer of a remote 713-acre tract of land on the island to establish a new monastery and a "manual labor school for colored boys." Three black brothers, the only members of Father Gabriel's community who did not go to Oklahoma, were to assist Father Oswald in his new endeavor. While the new buildings at Skidaway were being constructed, the small community remained at Isle of Hope where they received students for the new school in autumn of 1877. In June 1878, the monastic community occupied the newly completed buildings on Skidaway Island, which included a monastery, a dormitory for the students, and a storehouse. The school opened that spring with 12 students registered for the first term; there were 7 members of the monastic community residing at Skidaway at the time.

In 1879, Abbot Wimmer and Bishop Gross visited Father Oswald at Skidaway Island; there, it was decided that St. Vincent's should establish a "colored parish" in Savannah, like the earlier Benedictines had. It was decided that Father Oswald would serve as pastor of the new Sacred Heart Parish, while Fr. Melchior Reichert, OSB, would become superior of the monastery at Skidaway. Construction of the church was begun in October 1880, followed by a parish school in March 1882. In 1885, Mary Help Priory in Belmont, North Carolina, was elevated to the rank of abbey with the monasteries of Richmond, Virginia; and Skidaway Island, Georgia, as missions.

Grz. Abt Wimmer.

ABBOT BONIFACE WIMMER, OSB. In 1846, Boniface Wimmer and 18 monks from Bavaria established the first Benedictine monastery in the United States at St. Vincent, a small hamlet 40 miles southeast of Pittsburgh, Pennsylvania. Wimmer's original motivation for establishing the Benedictines in the United States was to provide equal religious opportunities for his countrymen, the thousands of German immigrants who had begun to establish themselves in America. Because most Catholic priests spoke languages other than German, Wimmer felt that the German-born Benedictine missionaries were the most suited to satisfy this need. Wimmer later expanded his evangelization to include other ethnicities, such as the Irish, Native Americans, and Eastern Europeans, in communities throughout the nation.

BISHOP WILLIAM H. GROSS, CSSR. In 1877, Abbot Wimmer accepted the request of Bishop William Gross of Savannah to minister to the freedmen "provided that the work harmonize with the principles of the Benedictine Order." (Courtesy of the Diocese of Savannah Archives & Records Management Office.)

FR. OSWALD MOOSEMUELLER, OSB. Oswald Moosemueller, Abbot Wimmer's most trusted administrator, established St. Benedict's Priory and Freedmen's School on Skidaway Island, founded Sacred Heart Parish, and negotiated the establishment of a permanent church for St. Benedict's Parish during his tenure in Savannah from 1877 to 1887. (Courtesy of the Diocese of Savannah Archives & Records Management Office.)

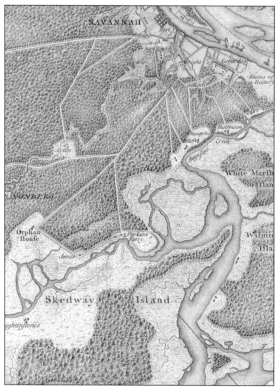

SKIDAWAY ISLAND, GEORGIA. Throughout history, Benedictine monasteries have been located in rural, pastoral settings as a means of maintaining self-sufficiency through farming, a hallmark of monastic life, while their remote locations promote a cloistered environment, as prescribed in the Rule of St. Benedict. Father Oswald favored establishing a new monastery and school at Skidaway Island because he hoped to become financially independent through farming its 713 acres "of which 300 acres are cleared land." (Courtesy of the Library of Congress.)

t. Benedicts Skidaway Island, Sav. Ga - Church & Monastery

ST. BENEDICT'S PRIORY, SKIDAWAY ISLAND, GEORGIA, CHURCH AND MONASTERY, C. 1880. The monastery and church, pictured here, were blessed on June 16, 1878, an occasion that was attended by over 600 guests who arrived from Savannah via a chartered boat. As monastic missions were expected to be self-sustaining, Father Oswald understood that the financial stability of the Skidaway foundation would depend on the ability of the community to maintain a viable and productive farm in the years to come. In lieu of tuition, which the poor black children they were tasked to educate could not afford, the monks would instead require their students to work the fields. According to historian Jerome Oetgen, the students' daily schedule was quite arduous, as the boys were roused from bed at "5 A.M., had Mass and meditation, worked for four hours during the day, received instructions for two hours, and recited the rosary twice daily with the brothers." As his correspondence reveals, Father Oswald intended to plant "40–50 acres of rice, corn, sweet potatoes, sugar cane, and sea-island cotton" in their first year on the island. Despite their efforts, the monastery farm was never very successful.

St. Benedict's Manual Labor School, Skidaway Island, Georgia, c. 1880. Students and their monk-instructors are pictured in front of the schoolhouse. Although the school enrolled an average of 10–12 students during the years it was open (1878–1889), it never received the community support that was necessary to sustain its long-term operation. Father Oswald wrote to Abbot Wimmer in August 1878 stating that the majority of blacks were not in favor of a manual labor school as "most have a horror of farm work" and that "they want their boys to get an education which fits them for positions of clerks, bookkeepers, and anything else but farmers." While the German-born Benedictines were not asking their charges to do anything that they themselves had not done as novices—most having worked the fields or performed other manual labor at St. Vincent's—as immigrants, Father Oswald and his confreres were not as sensitive to the circumstances of the former slaves as they needed to be. Only 15 years removed from slavery, the freedmen "identified manual labor and particularly farm labor with their former role as subservients," Oswald wrote.

BR. RHABANUS CONONGE, OSB, AND BROTHER ALOYSIUS, OSB. Br. Rhabanus Cononge (left) and Brother Aloysius (below) were both monks in residence at the monastery on Skidaway Island. Brother Rhabanus, the first black Benedictine in the Unites States, was from New Orleans. Brother Aloysius may have been one of the several local novices who joined the community during Father Oswald's tenure in Savannah. It was common for Benedictine missionaries to encourage local candidates to join the order. However, for these German-born Benedictines, it was crucial to their mission, as the Catholic Church in the United States did not allow blacks to be ordained as priests or to take vows to become nuns during this time. It was important to the success of the Benedictine mission that some of the monks were more culturally compatible to the local community they were serving. (Left, courtesy of St. Vincent Archabbey Archives; below, courtesy of Diocese of Savannah Archives & Records Management Office.)

Sacred Heart Church of the Benedictine Fathers in Savannah, Georgia.

SACRED HEART PARISH, C. 1884. This promotional postcard featuring an engraving of Sacred Heart Parish was used to solicit financial support for St. Vincent's missionary work among the freedmen in Savannah. In order to support both the monastery on Skidaway Island and the parish on Habersham Street, Father Oswald began publishing a German historical monthly, the *Gerschichtsfreund*, in 1880. With the funds raised from this publication, Father Oswald was able to cancel the debt on the church and to begin construction of a school for black children in 1882. The parish, which was located on the outskirts of the city where few blacks lived, began to attract white congregants from the developing suburb nearby. As a result, a new and larger school (at left) was built for white children soon thereafter. Father Oswald discontinued his publication in 1883 when subscriptions dropped sharply, effectively cutting off a major source of income for the black school. He was forced to close the school for blacks, and as a result, the parish become predominantly white by 1886.

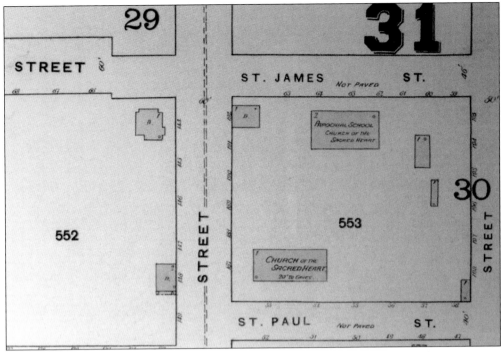

SACRED HEART CHURCH AND PAROCHIAL SCHOOL, C. 1888. The 1888 Sanborn fire insurance map shows the original location of Sacred Heart Parish along Habersham Street between St. James and St. Paul Streets (now Thirty-First and Thirty-Second Streets). The church was in the heart of the nascent Thomas Square neighborhood, a streetcar suburb that was largely settled by the burgeoning Irish middle class during the late 19th and early 20th centuries.

FR. MELCHIOR REICHERT, OSB, SUPERIOR OF ST. BENEDICT MONASTERY. Although Father Melchior, superior of the monastery at Skidaway, had achieved some initial success during the early 1880s, having increased enrollment at the school to 20 boys in 1882 and confirming numerous black converts in 1884, the mission was floundering financially by the late 1880s. In 1889, the monastery and school for black boys was closed, and the Benedictines withdrew from the island. (Courtesy of the Diocese of Savannah Archives & Records Management Office.)

MOTHER MATHILDA BEASLEY, FIRST BLACK NUN IN GEORGIA. Here is an undated image thought to be the only known photograph of Mother Mathilda Beasley. As a "free person of color," Mathilda Taylor arrived in Savannah in the 1850s and worked as a teacher and seamstress. In 1869, she married Abraham Beasley, a wealthy free black man who owned land and many businesses. After her husband's death in 1878, Mathilda embraced her faith and dedicated the rest of her life to her church and tending to the poor of her community. She donated all of the wealth she inherited from her husband to the Catholic Church, asking that a portion of the funds be used to establish an orphanage for black children. With the support of Father Oswald of Sacred Heart Church, Mathilda entered a Franciscan novitiate in York, England, in 1885. Sister Mathilda returned to Savannah, where she established the St. Francis Orphanage for Colored Children near Sacred Heart Church in 1887. In 1889, she formed the first community of African American nuns in Georgia in association with the Third Order of St. Francis. (Courtesy of the Diocese of Savannah Archives & Records Management Office.)

St. Benedict's Church, c. 1889, Mother Church of Black Catholics in Georgia. After more than a decade of enduring temporary quarters, the Benedictines built a new church, pictured here around 1930, solely for Savannah's black Catholics near the site of the original mission church. Having been crowded out at Sacred Heart, where they were relegated to meeting in the chapel, the new St. Benedict's would serve a congregation of 200; although, as reported by the *Savannah Morning News*, "there [were] 500 colored Catholics in the city." Father Melchior served as the first pastor.

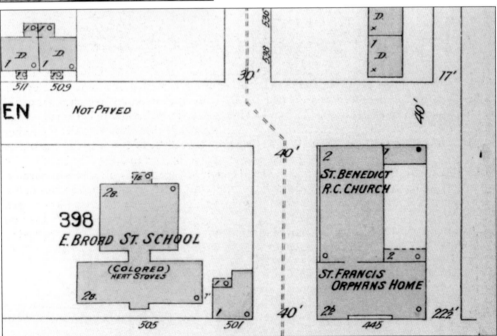

St. Benedict's Church, St. Francis Orphanage, c. 1898. The 1898 Sanborn fire insurance map shows the permanent location of St. Benedict's Church on the corner of East Gordon Lane and East Broad Street. During the late 1890s, St. Francis Orphanage was relocated to East Broad Street, where Mother Beasley continued to manage the facility until her partial retirement in 1899. After her death in 1903, the orphanage was operated by the Franciscan sisters who arrived in 1898 to assist her.

MOTHER MATHILDA BEASLEY COTTAGE. In 1901, Sacred Heart Church gave Mother Beasley this cottage, located on Price Street behind the church, so that the monks and parishioners could care for her in her old age. She was found dead in her cottage at the altar of her small private chapel on December 20, 1903, kneeling in prayer. An article titled "Died at Altar—Mother Beasley Found Dead in Her Private Chapel," was published the next day in the *Savannah Morning News* and attests to the high regard the people of Savannah had for her: "By the Sacred Heart clergy Mother Beasley was held in the highest esteem and only words of warmest praise and eulogy were heard concerning her. Protestants speak in the highest terms of her life and character, and among the negroes the feeling prevails that they have lost one of their best and truest friends and benefactors." Following a requiem Mass in a packed Sacred Heart Church, Mother Beasley was buried that morning. Her restored cottage was moved to Mother Mathilda Beasley Park across from St. Benedict the Moor Church in 2014.

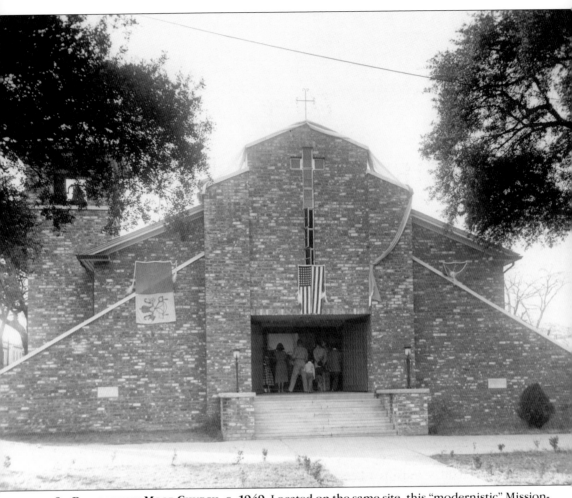

St. Benedict the Moor Church, c. 1949. Located on the same site, this "modernistic" Mission-style church replaced the earlier brick-and-frame church erected by the Benedictines in 1889. Although the Benedictines only remained in the parish for an additional seven years, ceding control of their apostolate to the Society of African Missions in 1907 (who renamed the parish St. Benedict the Moor), the founding of St. Benedict's Parish remains their most enduring legacy among Savannah's African American community during the 19th century.

Three

SACRED HEART PRIORY

Crescat *(Let it Grow)*

—Abbot Leo Haid, OSB

In 1902, Abbot Leo Haid reorganized his Savannah missions into a priory, consolidating his resources into a single primary apostolate centered on Sacred Heart Parish. As the monastic community and congregation had outgrown its existing quarters on Habersham Street, a new site was chosen at the corner of Bull and Thirty-Third Streets where a new monastic complex was built between 1902 and 1905.

The design for Sacred Heart Priory was a variation of the traditional rural cloister found at Belmont Abbey and called for a monastery, a parish church, and a boys' preparatory school, called Benedictine College. The compact arrangement of the buildings, in which the church and school flank the priory building on both sides, was intended to assure the appropriate monastic standards, while the close proximity of the monks' primary apostolates, the school and church, maintained the holy rule's tenet of restricting the monks' work to a cloistered setting.

A key difference in the Savannah monastery and the traditional monastic scheme lies in the location of the monastery within the city of Savannah and the establishment of Sacred Heart Church as a parish church. By accepting the responsibilities of a parish, the monks were accepting parochial duties rather than missionary duties. The monks would also be dependent on the Catholic laity of the parish to support their good works since the urban setting in which the priory was located made farming impossible (unlike the Skidaway Island foundation, which had only recently been abandoned).

Abbot Haid sent his most-gifted administrator, Fr. Bernard Haas, OSB, to implement his plan for Savannah, appointing him as the first prior of Sacred Heart Priory. Father Bernard, with the assistance of Fr. Aloysius O'Hanlon, OSB, pastor of Sacred Heart Church, opened Benedictine College in the fall of 1902 in temporary quarters on Habersham Street. The new church and priory were both completed in 1904, while the college building was completed and ready for use by the fall of 1905.

ABBOT LEO HAID, OSB, FIRST ABBOT OF BELMONT ABBEY. During his tenure as abbot of Belmont Abbey, North Carolina (1885–1922), Leo Haid established five monasteries in Virginia, Georgia, and Florida, each with its own college or school. According to Haid's biographer, Fr. Paschal Baumstein, OSB, "no single project of Abbot Leo's career ever matched the unqualified success of Bernard Haas and the priory, school, and parish in Savannah." (Courtesy of the Diocese of Savannah Archives & Records Management Office.)

SACRED HEART PARISH, C. 1900. This photograph, taken about 1900, is of the original Sacred Heart Church and parochial school (in background at left) on Habersham Street. As the congregation had outgrown the original frame missionary church by the turn of the 20th century, plans were made to build a larger church and a more permanent parish complex, a priory, on Bull Street. (Courtesy of the Diocese of Savannah Archives & Records Management Office.)

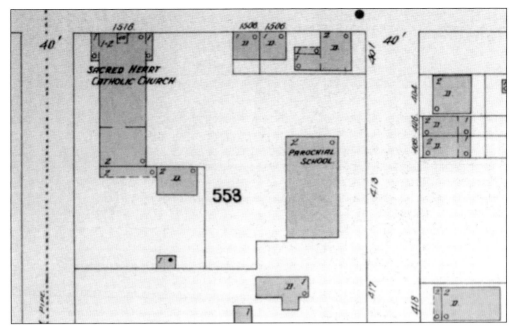

Sacred Heart Church and Parochial School, c. 1898. This Sanborn fire insurance map depicts the original parish church and school on Habersham Street between St. James and St. Paul Streets, four blocks east of the new Bull Street site. Building the new priory complex at a new site allowed the monks to continue the work of the parish uninterrupted until the new buildings were ready to occupy.

Benedictine College, c. 1902. Classes for Benedictine College were held in temporary quarters at the original Sacred Heart parochial school building, pictured here, on the corner of Habersham and St. James Streets, from 1902 through 1905. This photograph of the first class and faculty, titled "Bayonet Practice," was taken in 1902; Father Bernard, Col. Jordon F. Brooks, and Father Aloysius are pictured from left to right. (Courtesy of Belmont Abbey Archives.)

PATRICK JOSEPH "P.J." O'CONNOR, ESQUIRE. The portrait of P.J. O'Connor at left is from around 1905, and the photograph of the O'Connor family below was taken around 1890. A prominent local lawyer and city alderman, P.J. O'Connor, as well as his family, was an early member of Sacred Heart Parish. O'Connor was a respected community leader and organizer, serving as local, and later national, president of both the Ancient Order of Hibernians (AOH) and the Catholic Knights of America, societies he helped organize and establish in Savannah during the early 1880s. O'Connor played an instrumental role in the establishment of Sacred Heart Priory at its new site on Bull Street. As chairman of the church committee, O'Connor negotiated the purchase of the land, as well as the stained-glass windows, on behalf of Abbot Leo Haid. In addition, O'Connor used his considerable contacts in the community to help raise the funds for the construction of the church. (Both, courtesy of the O'Connor/Persse family.)

FATHER ALOYSIUS O'HANLON.

STREET ELEVATION, NEW SACRED HEART CH[...]

FACADE RENDERING OF SACRED HEART CHURCH, C. 1902.
The Benedictines engaged prominent local architect Hyman Whitcover to serve as supervising architect for the church and monastery. Whitcover's rendering of the church facade was published in the December 8 edition of the *Savannah Evening Press*. A photograph of Fr. Aloysius O'Hanlon, OSB, the pastor of Sacred Heart, was positioned above. (Courtesy of the O'Connor/Persse family.)

35

LAYING OF THE CORNERSTONE OF SACRED HEART CHURCH, C. 1902. Attended by three bishops, clergy, and several military and fraternal societies, the ceremony for the laying of the cornerstone of the new Sacred Heart Church and the blessing of the foundation was held on December 7, 1902. It was officiated by Bishop Keily of Savannah, who was assisted by his fellow bishops, Abbot Leo Haid, OSB, of Belmont, North Carolina, and Bishop Northrup of Charleston, South Carolina. The various Catholic societies in attendance, all of whom

marched in procession from Forsyth Park, included three divisions of the AOH, the Catholic Knights of America, and the Knights of Columbus. Leading the societies in their march, in perhaps their first official procession, were the recently formed Benedictine Cadets, who served as an honor guard. P.J. O'Connor's son Daniel was among the members of this first class of Benedictine College. (Courtesy of Sacred Heart Church.)

SACRED HEART CHURCH UNDER CONSTRUCTION, NOVEMBER 1904. Although the cornerstone and foundation were laid in 1902, construction was postponed until 1904 in order to raise the appropriate funds. The church, which was officially named Sacred Heart of Jesus, is a loose adaptation of the abbey church at Belmont Abbey. (Courtesy of Sacred Heart Church.)

MONASTERY, SACRED HEART PRIORY. This photograph of the monastery, or priory, was taken shortly after it was completed in 1904. A priory refers to both the rank of a monastery as well as the campus of monastery, church, and school in which it is situated. A priory is a monastery governed by a prior, who is in turn subject to the governance of the founding abbey, whereas an abbey is a monastery governed by an abbot. (Courtesy of Belmont Abbey Archives.)

BENEDICTINE COLLEGE, C. 1905. Architect Fr. Michael McInerny, OSB, a monk of Belmont Abbey, designed Benedictine College, which was among his first works. Initially charged by the abbey to oversee the progress of the lay architect, McInerny was later given the task of designing the new school building, which featured classrooms on the first floor and a large, open assembly area, called Benedictine Hall, on the second floor. (Courtesy of the Diocese of Savannah Archives & Records Management Office.)

SACRED HEART CATHOLIC CHURCH AND SCHOOL. This early 1900s postcard depicts Bull Street from its intersection with Thirty-Second Street; Sacred Heart Church and Benedictine College are in the distance. For many decades, the building on the right housed Gottlieb's Bakery, a staple for Sacred Heart parishioners and Benedictine Cadets alike. (Courtesy of the City of Savannah Research Library and Municipal Archives.)

SACRED HEART PRIORY, BULL STREET, C. 1905. Traditionally, a Benedictine daughter house often reflects the heritage of the founding abbey while also blending in characteristics indigenous to the area in which it is located. The buildings at Sacred Heart Priory exhibit a blend of Romanesque and German Gothic Revival that reflect the Bavarian origins of its motherhouse, Belmont Abbey. Materials native to Georgia, however, were used in the construction of all of the buildings: Ludowici clay tile for roofs, Augusta redbrick for exteriors, and Georgia granite and marble for trim. Because daughter houses are founded with the expectation that they will one day rise to the rank of abbey, it is important for each monastic foundation, architecturally and spiritually, to develop its own identity.

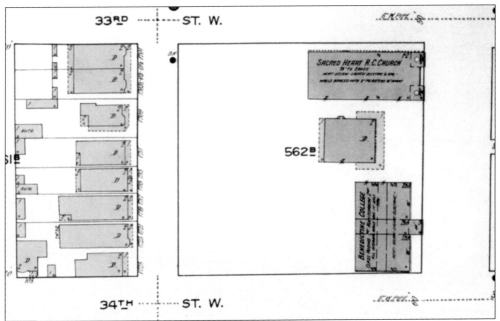

SACRED HEART PARISH COMPLEX, C. 1916. Sacred Heart Priory is depicted on this 1916 Sanborn fire insurance map. The compact arrangement of the buildings, in which the church and school flank the priory building on both sides, was meant to assure the appropriate monastic standards, while the close proximity of the monks' primary apostolates, the church and school, maintained the holy rule's tenet of restricting the monks' work to a cloistered setting.

DEDICATION PROCESSION, SACRED HEART CHURCH, C. 1905. On Sunday, February 19, 1905, the recently completed Sacred Heart of Jesus Catholic Church was formally dedicated. Here, numerous altar boys and priests process into the church at the beginning of the dedication ceremony while parishioners wait outside to take their seats. (Courtesy of Sacred Heart Church.)

DEDICATION OF SACRED HEART CHURCH AND PRIORY, C. 1905. Following the dedication of the church and the celebration of a solemn pontifical high Mass, distinguished clergymen from across the South and North who were in attendance, in addition to dozens of local clergy and Benedictine monks of Belmont Abbey and its several daughter houses, gathered for a reception at the new Sacred Heart Priory next door. This photograph of the clergy gathered there that day includes the Rt. Rev. Leo Haid, OSB, abbot of Belmont Abbey (on steps at center) surrounded by four bishops, from left to right, Rt. Rev. Bernard J. McQuaid, bishop of Rochester, New York; Rt. Rev. H.P. Northrup, bishop of Charleston, South Carolina; Rt. Rev. Benjamin J. Keily, bishop of Savannah; and Rt. Rev. William J. Kenny, bishop of St. Augustine.

Savannah, Ga., Sacred Heart Cathedral.

POSTCARD OF SACRED HEART CHURCH, C. 1905. Pictured here is a postcard of the church dating from the early 20th century. While the building is an imposing structure, with its towering spires and Gothic embellishment, Sacred Heart Church was never designated a cathedral, as this postcard erroneously states. (Courtesy of the City of Savannah Municipal Archives.)

Confirmation - Apr. 28, 1947

SACRED HEART CHURCH, C. 1947. This photograph of the interior of Sacred Heart Church was taken from the choir loft. One of the highlights of the church was its High Gothic–style altars, each of carved wood enameled in white and ornamented in gold leaf. In the center niche of the high altar stands a statue of the Sacred Heart. On the side niches below are a statue of St. Benedict, founder of the Order of St. Benedict, and his sister St. Scholastica, the founder of the Order of Benedictine Sisters. On each side of the high altar are the altar of the Blessed Virgin Mary, wherein stands a statue of Mary, Queen of Heaven, and the altar of St. Joseph. The church's Gothic arch stained-glass windows were designed and crafted by Francis Meyer and Company of the Royal Bavarian Institute in Munich, Germany, and are identical to those installed in the Abbey Church of Maryhelp (c. 1892) at Belmont Abbey. Each window depicts a saint of special significance to the Benedictine Order.

Four

BENEDICTINE COLLEGE

Come fall in line you men of old BC.

—Benedictine fight song

Begun as a boys' preparatory school, Benedictine College, as it was originally called, was organized on a military basis in the tradition of Southern military schools, like the Citadel and Virginia Military Institute. According to Abbot Haid's biographer, Fr. Paschal Baumstein, OSB, Haid included military training as part of the educational program for his new Savannah school because he believed a cadet corps provided "the environment that would best encourage the proper enrichment of youth." Haid believed that "a military program would develop the boy physically and mentally, and create habits of promptitude and order, foster self-reliance, and inculcate in the student, as part of his nature, manly ideas of obedience, loyalty, discipline, and courtesy." In adopting the prestigious military academy model for Benedictine College, the Savannah monks created an ordered and structured environment that promoted a disciplined approach to studies and virtue, an approach that complemented their own monastic lifestyle and aided in their overall goal of forming young men in body, mind, and soul.

Benedictine College opened in 1902 with 21 cadets and was an immediate success. By 1908, only its seventh year of operation, the school enrolled over 100 students, exceeding the student population of all the abbey's apostolates, even the school at Belmont. The Benedictine Cadets were highly visible in the community and often acted as a color guard or escort for civic occasions, as well as marching in the Savannah St. Patrick's Day Parade, an enduring tradition begun in 1903. The military aspect of the school appealed to the patriotic inclinations of Savannahians, and the community embraced the school as its own version of the Citadel. While Benedictine was established primarily to serve Savannah's young male Catholics, the school attracted non-Catholics as well, particularly the Jewish population and working-class Protestants, who shared an interest in the Judeo-Christian tradition of academic excellence, good moral living, respect for authority, and love of country.

TEMPORARY QUARTERS AT BENEDICTINE COLLEGE, C. 1902. Benedictine Cadets in formation present arms at the former Sacred Heart parish school on the corner of Habersham and St. James Streets. During the late 19th and early 20th centuries, colleges and secondary schools organized on a military basis were very fashionable in the South as a result of "traditional southern attitudes equating military service and martial valor with broader cultural notions of honor, patriotism, civic duty, and virtue," according to Ron Andrews in *Long Gray Lines: The Southern Military School Tradition 1839–1915*. An additional motivation may have been the government funds that schools qualified for under the Morrill Act of 1890 as a result of including military training as part of the curriculum. (Courtesy of the Diocese of Savannah Archives & Records Management Office.)

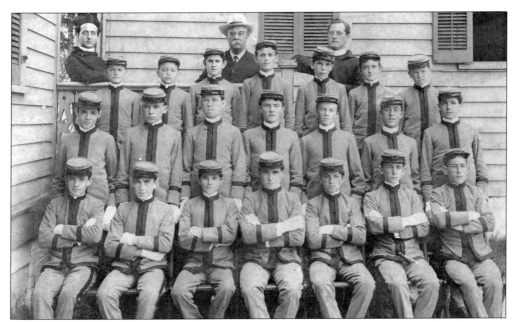

Students and Faculty of Benedictine College, c. 1902–1904. The photograph above shows the first class of 21 students to attend Benedictine College. Faculty members pictured are, from right to left, Fr. Bernard Haas, OSB, the first headmaster of the school and first prior of Sacred Heart Priory; Col. Jordon F. Brooks, military instructor and the school's first commandant; and Fr. Aloysius O'Hanlon, OSB, pastor of Sacred Heart Church from 1901 to 1908. In an identical pose as that of the 1902–1903 students, the photograph below shows the student body of Benedictine College for the 1903–1904 school year, which had grown to 32 pupils in just one year. Belmont Abbey accommodated this new growth with the assignment of an additional monk-professor, Fr. Jerome Finn, OSB, pictured third from left in the fourth row, for the newly formed Sacred Heart Priory.

BENEDICTINE COLLEGE MASQUERS, C. 1902–1904. Pictured here is an undated photograph of an acting troupe of cadets. Staging a play was likely the idea of Fr. Aloysius O'Hanlon, who was said to "share the abbot's love of the theater," according to Pashcal Baumstein. "He wrote plays, and even appeared as Hamlet." Like the monks of the abbey, some of the boys were compelled to take on female roles as the Benedictine College was an all-male environment.

CADET HENRY B. BRENNAN, CLASS OF 1919. This is a postcard portrait of cadet Henry B. Brennan wearing the cadet-gray uniform that was standard for many military academies of the period, most notably the Citadel. Cadet gray was worn at Benedictine College from 1902 until 1921, when it was replaced by the olive drab of the US Army.

STUDENTS AND FACULTY OF BENEDICTINE COLLEGE, 1905–1906. Above is the first photograph of the students and faculty of Benedictine College taken in front of the recently finished school building at the corner of Bull and Thirty-Fourth Streets in 1905. At the time, the school consisted of 37 students and five teachers. The following year, another photograph (below) was taken in a similar pose that illustrates the school's dramatic growth; by then, there were 56 cadets and 6 faculty members. New monks assigned to Sacred Heart Priory include Fr. Anthony Meyer, at far right in the second row, who arrived in Savannah in 1905.

BC CADETS FOOTBALL TEAM AND C. 1908 STUDENT BODY OF BENEDICTINE COLLEGE. The Benedictine College football team and coaches pictured above are in the side yard of the priory building on the Bull Street campus around 1909. Coach John Scott, who coached the team from 1905 to 1928, is at far right in the third row, with Fr. Jerome Finn, OSB, at center. According to Dom Paschal Baumstein, OSB, Abbot Leo Haid's biographer, the immediate success of the Savannah school, which exceeded 100 students in 1908 (below), compared to the meager attendance of his own St. Mary's College at Belmont, was a source of irritation for Haid. In addition, Paschal reveals that Abbot Haid, in discussing the affairs of the abbey's many dependencies throughout the South, was "annoyed" to report that Benedictine College had gained "an increasing reputation that centered on the boys' good looks and football."

ST. PATRICK'S DAY PARADE. These early photographs show the Benedictine Cadets marching in the parade in 1911 (above) and 1930 (below). During the early 1900s, the cadets were well known in Savannah and were often asked to take part in various civic occasions, ceremonies, and military observances. However, the Corps of Cadets is best known for its annual participation in Savannah's St. Patrick's Day Parade. This tradition was begun by P.J. O'Connor, the president of Division One of the AOH, which was affiliated with Sacred Heart Church. Fr. Aloysius O'Hanlon, OSB, the pastor of Sacred Heart, served as division and county chaplain for the AOH during the early 1900s. During the early years of the school's development, the cadets served as an honor guard for the AOH in the parade.

FACULTY OF BENEDICTINE COLLEGE, C. 1909. Faculty of Benedictine College outside the entrance to Sacred Heart Church are, from left to right, Fr. Ambrose Gallagher, OSB; Fr. Jerome Finn, OSB; unidentified; Fr. Bernard Haas, OSB, prior; Col. Jordan F. Brooks, commandant; Fr. Cornelius Diehl, OSB; and Fr. Anthony Meyer, OSB. (Courtesy of Belmont Abbey Archives.)

MEMBERS OF THE BENEDICTINE COLLEGE BASEBALL TEAM, C. 1918. Benedictine College baseball players pose for a photograph on the steps of the priory. In addition to football, Benedictine College offered the cadets the opportunity to play other sports, such as baseball, cross country, and basketball. Coach John Scott, who was brought on to coach football in 1905, coached many of the teams during his tenure.

COLLAGE OF BC CADETS ON DRILL FIELD, C. 1900s. The 1909 Benedictine College school catalogue features two photograph collages of the cadets marching on the drill/exercise field behind the school, a half-block parcel of land fronting Whitaker Street between East Thirty-Third and Thirty-Fourth Streets.

DRILL EXHIBITION, BENEDICTINE COLLEGE CAMPUS, 1910s. The 1919 school catalogue features this photograph of the Benedictine Cadets on the drill field behind the college building during an exhibition as the public looks on. The following text about the military training the cadets receive is from a school catalogue of the period:

> All students are required to wear the uniform and to take military training which is designed to teach such features of discipline as obedience, promptness, neatness, and self-reliance, as will be of value in any walk of life. The daily drill period is short and the program carried out is necessarily limited, but all Cadets are thoroughly instructed in the school of the company and battalion, extended order, guard duty, ceremonies and hygiene, and given physical exercises and actual target firing on the Government rifle range."

President Taft et B.C.

PRES. HOWARD TAFT ADDRESSING THE BENEDICTINE CADETS, C. 1912. In 1912, President Taft came to Savannah, where he stayed at the home of his fellow Yale classmate, Gen. William W. Gordon, father of Girl Scout founder Juliette Gordon-Low. According to the *Savannah Morning News*, Taft's motorcade made a scheduled stop in front of Benedictine College, where he was met by the cadets at present arms. Taft made a five-minute speech in which he recommended that the cadets "never forget the poise and bearing that military training gives you" and instructed them to carry with them in life "the principles of discipline which you have learned in a military institution." (Courtesy of Belmont Abbey Archives.)

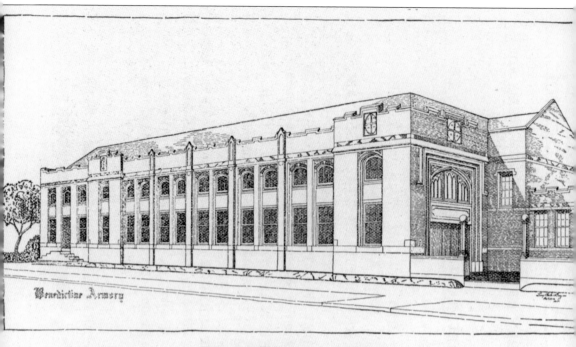

THE BENEDICTINE ARMORY

An Armory is now under construction. It will be opened in September. It is built of red brick with limestone trimmings and measures 178x62. Contains gun-rack room, toilets, auditorium, stage, showers and dressing room

CLETUS W. BERGEN, AMERICAN INSTITUTE OF ARCHITECTS (AIA), "DEAN OF SAVANNAH ARCHITECTS," CLASS OF 1912. Cletus Bergen was one of the most prolific and influential architects in Savannah during the 20th century. After graduating from Benedictine, Bergen attended architecture school at Georgia Tech, where he graduated in 1919. He began his career with the firm of Levy and Clark, where one of the first buildings he designed was for the Benedictines in 1921, Sacred Heart Grammar School on Abercorn Street, the priory's newest apostolate. In 1925, the Benedictines engaged Bergen to design a new armory/gymnasium (pictured), which was to be built behind the college building. He opened his own office in 1927 and went on to become known as the "dean of architects" in Savannah, as most of the city's major architects began their careers in his office. His most notable designs include the Central of Georgia Railroad Conductor's Home (Oatland Island, c. 1926), Battey Street School (Charles Ellis, c. 1928), Gould Cottage (c. 1931), Charity Hospital (c. 1931), Savannah High School (c. 1935), Savannah Fire Department Headquarters Building (c. 1936), Henry Ford House (Richmond Hill, c. 1936), St. Mary's Home (c. 1937), and Our Lady of Lourdes Catholic Church (Port Wentworth, c. 1940).

CADETS IN FORMATION, C. 1919. These two photographs, which show the student body of Benedictine College lined up at parade rest on the drill field, are actually sections of a larger panorama of the campus. School catalogs of the period list the day order: "8:30 A.M. – doors open; 8:45 – Raising National Colors by Color Detail; 8:55 A.M. – Roll Call; 9:00 A.M. – Military Drill; 9:20 A.M. – Recitation, Mathematics, Latin and Greek, Geography, etc.; 11:30 A.M. – Recess; 12 to 2 P.M. – Recitation, English, Penmanship. Elocution, Commercial Law, Shorthand, etc.; 2:00 P.M. – National Colors lowered."

BENEDICTINE COLLEGE ROLL OF HONOR, C. 1918. *Roll of Honor,* which today hangs in Alumni Hall, is the work of well-known Savannah artist Christopher Murphy Sr., who created the painting to honor the alumni of Benedictine College who fought in World War I. The 206 veterans of the war, which represents nearly half of the students who attended Benedictine from 1902 until 1917, are listed along with the seven cadets who died in the line of duty. Murphy's son Christopher A.D. Murphy was a student at Benedictine at the time that this painting was presented to the school. The younger Murphy, who graduated from Benedictine in 1921, became a well-known artist in his own right and was known professionally as Christopher Murphy Jr.

MSGR. PATRICK J. O'CONNOR JR., BC CLASS OF 1920. Promising actor Patrick J. O'Connor Jr. is pictured at right in a promotional photograph for a national touring company around 1925. According to *Southern Cross* columnist Rita H. DeLorme, O'Connor "was on his way to a successful career in Hollywood or on Broadway in 1924 when he entered theatrical producer Max Gordon's American Academy of Dramatic Arts," signing "a three-year contract to play the RKO Orpheum Circuit, a training program for up-and-coming actors." Yet two years into the coast-to-coast tour, O'Connor left acting to enter the priesthood. He was ordained for the Diocese of Savannah in 1933. Like his father P.J., O'Connor was a gifted orator and, over a career that spanned four decades, was, according to DeLorme, "internationally known as an eloquent preacher and lecturer." His service to the church was well regarded and gained him wide recognition. He is pictured below meeting Pope Pius XII. (Both, courtesy of the Persse family.)

CHRISTOPHER MURPHY JR., CLASS OF 1921. Christopher A.D. Murphy (first row, far left) poses with his fellow graduates on the priory steps around 1921. Murphy was born into a well-known family of Savannah artists who encouraged his studies at the Art Students League in New York City, where he moved shortly after graduation. During the 1920s, Murphy divided his time between Savannah and New York, studying painting and composition, portraiture, etching, and architecture with various mentors. His etchings, such as *Joe Street, Savannah*, (below), and portraits won awards, and his work was widely exhibited, appearing in museums and art galleries in London, New York, Philadelphia, and Chicago. During the 1930s and the decades thereafter, Murphy orchestrated his career from Savannah, maintaining a rigorous exhibition schedule. He remained an advocate of the arts through his association with the Savannah Art Club and the Association of Georgia Artists, teaching locally at the Telfair Museum of Arts and Sciences and Armstrong State College. (Below, Christopher A.D. Murphy, *Joe Street, Savannah*, Undated. Charcoal on paper. Morris Museum of Art, Augusta, Georgia, and with permission of the artist's son Christopher Cole Murphy.)

DIFFERENT LEVELS, CHRISTOPHER MURPHY. Christopher Murphy was a prominent 20th-century artist, teacher, and arts advocate in Savannah. He was best known for his etchings of his native city and the surrounding area. According to art historian and author Karen Towers Klacsmann, Murphy liked to sketch outdoors: "Captivated with Savannah's distinctive architecture and familiar with its landmarks, he systematically captured the ebb and flow of daily life in the streets and on the waterfront from 1925 until his death. Acutely aware of changes brought about by both progress and neglect, Murphy visited deserted historic plantations with crumbling outbuildings and wandered into rural areas outside the city, drawing what he saw." *Different Levels* (above) is one of 37 illustrations Murphy drew for the book *Savannah* (c. 1947), written by historian Walter C. Hartridge, the first president of the Historic Savannah Foundation. *Savannah* was well received and helped draw attention to the city's nascent historic preservation efforts. (Christopher A.D. Murphy, *Different Levels*, Undated. Graphite on paper. Morris Museum of Art, Augusta, Georgia. Gift of the Robert Powell Coggins Art Trust, and with permission of the artist's son Christopher Cole Murphy.)

THE GRADUATES

BENEDICTINE SCHOOL. Pictured here is a montage using the individual photographs of each of the graduates of the class of 1924 to form the initials "BC." In 1921, the school's administration decided to change its name from Benedictine College to Benedictine School in order to better define its mission as a preparatory school. Despite the name change, the school continued to be referred to by its well-known abbreviation, "BC."

CADET JOHN R. STARRS, CLASS OF 1927. Pictured is Senior Cadet Lieutenant John R. Starrs wearing the olive-drab uniform that was standard for the US Army. The change from the cadet grays to standard Army-issued uniforms coincided with the efforts of the school's new commandant, Capt. Edward J. Thomson, to align the military program with the nation's new Junior Reserve Officer Training Program (JROTC). The olive-drab uniform was worn from 1922 to 1930.

The *Cadet*, c. 1924. Pictured is the inner sleeve of the *Cadet*, Benedictine School's first yearbook. The image of a cadet blowing a bugle is accompanied by an emblem of an eagle straddling an open book bearing the letters "BC," its talons holding a ribbon bearing the inscription "UIOGD," which is the Latin acronym for the Benedictine motto "So that in all things may God be glorified."

Third Academic, Benedictine School, c. 1924. This photograph of the third academic was taken on the steps of the priory; note that the cadets arranged their service caps in the shape of a "B" on the sidewalk in front of them. While the terms freshman, sophomore, junior, and senior are often used to indicate grade levels, first academic, second academic, and so on were used at this time instead.

BENEDICTINE ARMORY, C. 1925. In 1925, Benedictine Armory was built off the rear of the college building, providing the cadets with new locker rooms, a gun room, and an auditorium that doubled as a basketball court. Benedictine Hall, which was located on the second floor of the college building, was converted into classrooms for the growing student population. The new building was modeled after the academy building at West Point. (Courtesy of the Diocese of Savannah Archives & Records Management Office.)

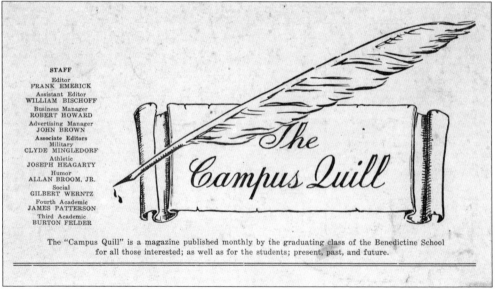

THE CAMPUS QUILL, C. 1927. Pictured is the masthead of the first issue of *The Campus Quill*, a school newsletter published monthly by the graduating class of Benedictine School. The first edition was dedicated to Fr. Bernard Haas, OSB, rector of BC from 1902 until 1919, who had recently suffered a debilitating heart attack. *The Campus Quill* was published through the late 1940s and was later renamed *The Benedictine Cadet.*

GOV. AL SMITH OF NEW YORK, C. 1928. The Benedictine Cadets are at parade rest in the front yard of the priory as the monks receive Governor Smith of New York, the Democratic Party's candidate for president in 1928. Smith was the first Catholic to be nominated for president by a major political party. He won Georgia's electoral votes, but lost the presidency to Republican Herbert Hoover.

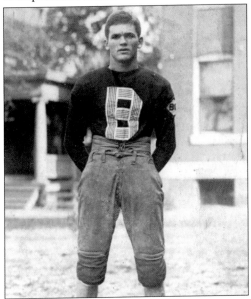

BENEDICTINE FOOTBALL TEAM, 1920S. Unidentified football players pose on the exercise/drill field at the back of the campus. In addition to playing Savannah High School, BC's traditional rival, Benedictine often played teams from neighboring counties as there was a limited number of local schools with football teams during the 1920s. In an effort to find opponents, it was common for BC to play the freshman squad of colleges such as the Citadel, Oglethorpe, and South Carolina.

CADET GRILEY, 1930s. Cadet underclassman Griley wears dress whites, the standard uniform at Benedictine from 1931 to 1967. The uniform consists of a blue "blouse" (coat) and white pants and gloves for formal occasions and blue pants with black stripe for everyday wear. The cross belts with brass buckle shown here were worn by non-officers, while brown leather belts with maroon sash were worn by officers.

BC BASKETBALL TEAM, THE MAROONS, C. 1930–1931. Members of the 1930 BC basketball team are, from left to right, Maj. Wadsworth Crawford, manager; Charles Traynor; Mazo; Frank Rossiter; John Trapani; Robert Carr; David Center; John Davis; Richard Dolan; Reid Canty, captain; and coach Francis X. O'Keefe. By this time, Benedictine was also fielding tennis and track teams.

Lt. Col. T. Nugent Courvoisie, "the Boo," Class of 1934. Thomas Nugent Courvoisie, pictured above second from left in the first row, graduated from Benedictine in 1934. A 1952 graduate of the Citadel, Courvoisie served in the military from 1938 to 1961 and was a veteran of World War II and the Korean War. From 1961 to 1968, he served as assistant commandant of cadets in charge of discipline at the Citadel. He was affectionately referred to as "the Boo" by the cadets, who he called his "lambs." In 1980, Pat Conroy immortalized Courvoisie in his best-selling book *The Lords of Discipline*. Conroy's character, Col. "Bear" Berrineau, was based on Courvoisie and was a "tough talking, cigar chomping molder of men." Conroy described Courvoisie as being "many things to many people . . . he was part analyst, part confessor, part detective, part father, part son of a bitch, and all soldier." (Below, courtesy of the Citadel Archives and Museum.)

Lt. Gen. John N. McLaughlin, US Marine Corps, Class of 1936. Cadet Captain John McLaughlin graduated from Benedictine in 1936. During a military career that spanned nearly four decades, McLaughlin was a highly decorated officer of the US Marine Corps who served in the Pacific during World War II, in Korea, and in Vietnam. In 1950, he was taken prisoner by the Chinese during the Korean War and spent three years in captivity, serving much of this time as senior officer in command among the prisoners of war in the camp. During the Vietnam War, then Brigadier General McLaughlin was assigned to Danang in 1968 and served as the assistant division commander of the 1st Marine Division as well as the commander of Task Force X Ray during the Tet Offensive. After the war, McLaughlin was appointed commanding general of Marine Corps Recruit Depot, San Diego, and later assumed command of the 4th Marine Division at Camp Pendleton. He finished his career as commanding general of Fleet Marine Force, Pacific, the largest field command in the Marine Corps, which he held until his retirement in 1977. (Courtesy of US Marine Corps Military History Division.)

Five

Parish and Community Life

UTIOGD (Latin acronym for "So that in all things God may be glorified")

—Benedictine motto

The establishment of Sacred Heart Priory on Bull Street during the early 1900s allowed the Benedictines to consolidate their efforts in one location and concentrate on the success of their primary apostolates—the parish church, Sacred Heart, and the monastery school, Benedictine College. In addition to their parochial duties, which included the celebration of Mass several times a day as well as the administration of the sacraments, the monks shared teaching duties at the school while also maintaining their observance of the divine office, the foundation of Benedictine life. With the early and unequaled success of Benedictine College, additional monks from Belmont Abbey were assigned to the growing priory, which allowed the monks to expand their service to the community and for the establishment of new apostolates.

In 1908, the Benedictines reopened Our Lady of Good Hope Chapel at Isle of Hope, which became a mission of Sacred Heart Parish for over 60 years. The reopening of the mission chapel was followed by the acceptance of chaplain duties at numerous local convents, monasteries, schools, and hospitals over the course of several decades, including, but not limited to, the Little Sisters of the Poor, Sacred Heart Convent (Sisters of St. Joseph of Carondelet), St. Mary's Home, St. Joseph's Hospital, Reidsville State Penitentiary, and the Carmelite Monastery.

In 1916, Sacred Heart Priory established a coed grade school, Sacred Heart Grammar School, in a converted apartment house on the corner of Abercorn and East Thirty-Eighth Streets. In 1922, the apartment house was replaced with a new, two-story brick school building.

In 1925, the priory built an armory for the benefit of Benedictine College. However, the building was also used by the parish grammar school children for sports and theatrical productions and by Sacred Heart Church as a parish meeting hall.

Sacred Heart Priory established the mission chapels of St. James the Less on the south side of Savannah in 1949 and St. Ann's in Richmond Hill in 1955. Both missions grew into full parish churches serving the Diocese of Savannah.

Our Lady of Good Hope Chapel, 1908–1969. The photograph above is of the interior of the refurbished chapel at Isle of Hope and was taken from the choir loft. In 1908, the Benedictines of Sacred Heart Priory reopened Our Lady of Good Hope Chapel, where they served Isle of Hope's Catholic community for the next 60 years. The chapel remained a mission of Sacred Heart Parish until 1970, when diocesan priests assumed responsibility. Today, the chapel (below) is maintained by St. James Church, whose parishioners renovated the building in 1974 to commemorate the 100th anniversary of the arrival of Benedictines in Savannah. (Above, courtesy of the Diocese of Savannah Archives & Records Management Office; below, author photograph.)

GROUND BREAKING AT SACRED HEART GRAMMAR SCHOOL, C. 1921. Above, Fr. Eugene Egan, OSB, (center) prior of the Benedictine Community in Savannah and pastor of Sacred Heart Church, breaks ground at the site of the new Sacred Heart Grammar School at the corner of Abercorn and East Thirty-Eighth Streets. The apartment house in the background was remodeled in 1916 to serve as a temporary school building while a second apartment building on the site (not visible) served as a convent for the Sisters of St. Joseph of Carondelet who were placed in charge of the school. Designed by local architect Cletus Bergen, a 1912 graduate of Benedictine College, the new two-story brick school building (below) was completed in 1922. (Above, courtesy of Sacred Heart Church; below, courtesy of the Diocese of Savannah Archives & Records Management Office.)

SACRED HEART CONVENT, C. 1930. Pictured is Sacred Heart Convent on the corner of Abercorn and East Thirty-Seventh Streets. In 1925, the Benedictines purchased the old Owens House to serve as a new, more suitable convent for the Sisters of St. Joseph of Carondelet. As part of the renovation, a new two-story wing was added on the rear of the building, which included a residence hall on the first floor and a chapel (below) on the second floor. The Benedictine monks of Sacred Heart Priory served as chaplains to the sisters for over 40 years, assuming responsibility for the convent chapel until the late 1960s. (Courtesy of the Diocese of Savannah Archives & Records Management Office.)

THIRD GRADE, SACRED HEART GRAMMAR SCHOOL, C. 1945–1946. The third-grade class of Sacred Heart Grammar School poses on the steps of the school building. While the Sisters of St. Joseph served as the principal administrators and primary teachers, the school was an apostolate of Sacred Heart Priory, the parish school. As such, the monks were a frequent presence, teaching religion classes as well as preparing the children for the sacraments. (Courtesy of the Diocese of Savannah Archives & Records Management Office.)

GRADUATING CLASS OF SACRED HEART GRAMMAR SCHOOL, C. 1946. This photograph of the graduating class of Sacred Heart Grammar School, Bishop Hyland, monks of Sacred Heart Priory, and altar boys was taken on the steps of the priory following the graduation ceremony, which was likely held in the church following Mass. (Courtesy of the Diocese of Savannah Archives & Records Management Office.)

Our Lady of Good Hope Chapel, 1940s. This photograph of the chapel was taken from the choir loft during Mass. Before the 1930s, monks from Sacred Heart Church would travel to Isle of Hope by streetcar to say Mass at the chapel on Sunday mornings. Since it was such a long trip, Catholic families on the island would take turns hosting the priests for breakfast after the second Mass. The little chapel has served generations of Isle of Hope families. (Courtesy of the Diocese of Savannah Archives & Records Management Office.)

Confirmation at Sacred Heart Grammar School, 1940s. Taken from the choir loft of Sacred Heart Church, this 1940s photograph shows students from Sacred Heart Grammar School, perfectly aligned in the pews, listening to Bishop Hyland during their Confirmation Mass. While many of the monks of Sacred Heart Priory were assigned teaching duties at Benedictine, the whole monastic community took part in the spiritual development of the parish's youth. (Courtesy of the Diocese of Savannah Archives & Records Management Office.)

MISSION CHAPEL OF ST. JAMES THE LESS, MAY DAY, C. 1950. At right, Fr. Terrance Kernan, OSB (left), and Fr. Bede Lightner, OSB, pose with altar boys and neighborhood children on the steps of the new mission chapel of St. James the Less on Whitfield Avenue following the annual May Day crowning, pictured below. Father Terrance, who was in charge of Our Lady of Good Hope Chapel at nearby Isle of Hope, petitioned the Diocese of Savannah-Atlanta in 1949 for permission to establish a new mission on the city's burgeoning suburban south side to meet the needs of the growing Catholic community. The diocese purchased the land, and a surplus US Air Force chapel was moved to the site in time for the first Mass on Christmas Day 1949. (Both, courtesy of the Diocese of Savannah Archives & Records Management Office.)

First Communion at St. James the Less Parish, c. 1959. Fr. John Toomey, altar boys, and children of the new parish of St. James the Less pose on the steps of the church following First Communion Mass, April 5, 1959. St. James the Less Chapel was a mission of the Benedictines of Sacred Heart Church from 1949 to 1956 and was under the care of Father Kernan, OSB. (Courtesy of the Diocese of Savannah Archives & Records Management Office.)

Confirmation Class, Sacred Heart Grammar School, c. 1959. The 1959 Confirmation class of Sacred Heart Grammar School poses with Fr. Terrance Kernan, OSB, on the steps of the school building. After serving as the founding pastor of the St. James mission, Father Terrance became the pastor of Sacred Heart Church, an office he held until 1969. (Courtesy of the Diocese of Savannah Archives & Records Management Office.)

76

Six

BENEDICTINE MILITARY SCHOOL

For God, Country, and Benedictine

—BC motto

While the military school tradition began to fade elsewhere in the South following the federal government's introduction of the ROTC program in 1916, the military aspect at BC accelerated, and the identity of the school became forever intertwined with that of its monastic community. Emblematic of this is the adoption of a shoulder sleeve insignia consisting of Abbot Leo Haid's coat of arms as a standard part of the cadet's uniform—with the lion representing Haid, the first abbot of Belmont Abbey—and the 10 stars representing the first monks who accompanied him from St. Vincent's to North Carolina. In 1933, the Benedictine Cadets were afforded the special distinction of serving as an honor guard for Pres. Franklin Delano Roosevelt's motorcade upon his arrival and departure from Municipal Stadium in Daffin Park where he addressed the crowd during Georgia's bicentennial celebration. In 1936, Benedictine became the first day military school in the nation to become an honor unit of distinction, prompting the monks to change the name of the school to Benedictine Military School the following year. Despite these accolades, the active participation of hundreds of Benedictine graduates in the US Armed Forces during World War II, as well as a number of students enrolled at the school who left early to enlist, was the singular event in the history of the school and its monastic community that solidified the military-religious identity of the Savannah monastery-school. A memorial to the 30 Benedictine graduates and current students who died in the line of duty was erected on the Benedictine campus in 1947 to honor their memory and sacrifice to their country.

By the 1950s, it had become a tradition among Savannah families for sons to attend the alma mater of their fathers and grandfathers. With enrollment skyrocketing and the old college building, constructed to accommodate 200 students, no longer suiting the growing needs of the school and monastic community, the monks of Sacred Heart Priory began to plan for the construction of a new suburban campus on Savannah's south side, purchasing a wooded 99-acre tract in 1958, the same year that the priory received a bequest of $500,000.

SHOULDER SLEEVE INSIGNIA, c. 1937. This shoulder sleeve insignia was a standard part of the Benedictine Cadet's uniform from 1937 to 2014. While the US Army Institute of Heraldry approved the insignia in 1931, it was not worn until after Benedictine applied for and received admission into the ROTC program in 1935. A year after being rated an honor unit of distinction, the shoulder sleeve insignia was introduced in 1937, the same year that the name of the school was changed to Benedictine Military School. As worn by Cadet Master Sergeant Gilbert A. Maggioni in the photograph below, the stars and lion are set on a field of red.

William P. "Billy" Bergen, AIA, Class of 1939. At right is a photograph of Cadet Lieutenant William P. Bergen, son of architect Cletus Bergen (class of 1912). Following distinguished military service in World War II, Bergen, like his father before him, graduated from the School of Architecture at Georgia Tech and joined his father's architectural practice in 1948. One of Billy Bergen's first commissions was the landmark design for the Drayton Arms Apartments (c. 1949), an iconic International-style building that is today regarded as one of the best examples of Modernism in Georgia (below). Other notable designs include the Savannah Home for Girls (c. 1950), Country Day School (c. 1956), Fire Station No. 1 (Paulson Street, c. 1958), Blessed Sacrament School (c. 1958), WSAV Studios (Victory Drive, c. 1959), and St. James School (c. 1960). (Below, courtesy of the City of Savannah Municipal Archives on behalf of V. & J. Duncan Antique Maps and Prints.)

Drayton Arms Apartments
Savannah, Georgia

SSGT. GEORGE K. GANNAM, CLASS OF 1938. US Army Staff Sergeant Gannam poses in uniform around 1940. On December 7, 1941, Sergeant Gannam, a 1938 graduate of Benedictine, was the first Savannahian killed in World War II during the Japanese surprise attack on Pearl Harbor. News of Gannam's death and his heroic actions during the attack reached Savannah on December 11. The city gathered to pay tribute to Gannam the following day at a requiem Mass (below) at Sacred Heart Church, his parish church, which was attended by the entire student body of Benedictine Military School. These images are part of the scrapbook compiled by the Gannam family following his death. (Both, courtesy of the City of Savannah Municipal Archives.)

FLAG-RAISING CEREMONY AT THE GANNAM RESIDENCE, FEBRUARY 1942. A few months after Gannam's requiem Mass, buglers from the senior class at Benedictine, accompanied by a detail of cadets, participated in a flag-raising ceremony at the Gannam residence on the corner of West Fifty-Third and Hopkins Streets, which was attended by monks of Sacred Heart Priory and faculty of Benedictine Military School. A new flagpole, recently erected by George's father, was dedicated as part of a small memorial garden planted by the family. This small intimate ceremony (above), in which a wreath was placed at the base of the flagpole and the national colors were raised (below), followed by Taps, was repeated at the Gannam home on the anniversary of the attack on Pearl Harbor for several years. This ceremony eventually evolved into what is now known as Gannam Day at BC. (Both, courtesy of the City of Savannah Municipal Archives.)

BENEDICTINE AWARDED CHARTER IN VICTORY CORPS, C. 1943. In 1943, as a result of the school's civic presence and contributions to the war effort, Benedictine was awarded a charter in the Victory Corps, a national high school organization for the promotion of war activities. The four years of military training and tactics that each cadet received as a standard part of the educational program at BC made the members of the Corps of Cadets ideal candidates for the armed services, a call to duty that was answered by many of the school's alumni. The award was made to the student body of Benedictine "for its active and vigorous participation in the promotion of activities relating to national defense and victory." The cadets often took part in training exercises at military bases, like the Marine Corps Recruit Depot at Parris Island, South Carolina, as seen in these photographs from 1947.

OSCAR C. BURNETT, OSB, SEVENTH ABBOT OF BELMONT ABBEY, CLASS OF 1944. At right is Cadet First Sergeant Oscar C. Burnett Jr. in a photograph taken for his senior class composite. Burnett and his family were parishioners of Sacred Heart Church, where he attended the parish school, Sacred Heart Grammar School, before graduating from Benedictine in 1944. Burnett served in the US Army Air Force during World War II before attending Emory University in Macon, where he earned a degree in law. He practiced law in Savannah for six years before entering the novitiate at Belmont Abbey, professing his vows in 1958. He was ordained to the priesthood in 1962. At Belmont Abbey College, "the Big O," as he was known to the students, held a number of positions over the years, including associate professor, dean of students, and president and chancellor of the college. His service to the monastic community included the offices of subprior, procurator, pastor of the abbey parish, novice master, and prior. He was elected abbot in 1991 and served until 1999. (Below, courtesy of Belmont Abbey Archives.)

ST. PATRICK'S DAY PARADE, C. 1946. The Benedictine Cadets march down Bull Street during the St. Patrick's Day Parade. Because so many of Savannah's men were off fighting overseas, the annual St. Patrick's Day Parade was not held between 1942 and 1945. However, a truncated version of the parade, with the cadets acting as the sole traditional unit, was held during these years, continuing one of Savannah's longest traditions.

GANNAM DAY, DECEMBER 7, 1945. What could be considered the first Gannam Day ceremony was held at the Gannam home in 1945 on the fourth anniversary of the attack on Pearl Harbor. On this occasion, the entire BC Corps of Cadets was in attendance for the first time along with the newly formed George K. Gannam American Legion Post No. 184, which directed the memorial services and laid a wreath at the foot of the flagpole. (Courtesy of the City of Savannah Municipal Archives.)

BENEDICTINE VERSUS SAVANNAH HIGH SCHOOL, THANKSGIVING DAY FOOTBALL GAME. BC head football coach Jim Fordham (crouching above) and staff watch from the sidelines in Grayson Stadium as the Cadets play their archrivals, the Savannah High School Blue Jackets, on Thanksgiving Day 1946. According to BC historian Maurice Sheppard (class of 1955), the Thanksgiving Day Football Classic was played from 1920 to 1959. All of the games from 1941 to 1959 were played in Grayson Stadium. After World War II, interest in the game increased dramatically, with attendance sometimes reaching as many as 15,000. Savannah High went on to beat Benedictine 27-6 in the 1946 match.

DEDICATION AND UNVEILING OF WAR MEMORIAL, APRIL 25, 1947. The photograph above is of the bishop of the Diocese of Savannah-Atlanta, Francis Edward Hyland, addressing the assembled crowd during the dedication of the war memorial. By 1945, more than a dozen Benedictine graduates had joined Sergeant Gannam in the ranks of "BC Heroes," and plans were made to erect a memorial on the Benedictine campus to honor their memory and sacrifice to their country. Clearly influenced by the Gannam memorial garden, the memorial consisted of a newly paved concrete plaza with a limestone monument surrounding the base of the campus flagstaff with the names of all of the fallen cadets inscribed. At the dedication ceremony, Father Bede read the names of the honored dead, which was followed by the unveiling of the monument by the families of the fallen (below), a volley salute by the firing squad, Taps, and the lowering of the colors.

FAMILIES OF THE HONORED DEAD, DEDICATION OF MEMORIAL, C. 1947. The photograph of the families above was taken during the dedication of the World War II War Memorial. The names of their fallen sons, brothers, and classmates were inscribed on a marble plaque embedded in the limestone monument that surrounded the campus flagstaff, as seen below. By the time of the dedication of the monument, 30 cadets had been killed in action during the war. The young cadet in the photograph above is standing in the front row next to his father as his older brother's name is called during the dedication ceremony.

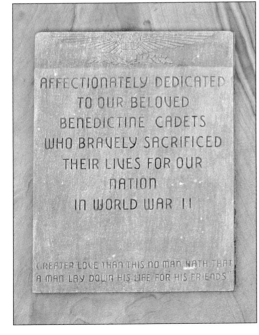

AFFECTIONATELY DEDICATED
TO OUR BELOVED
BENEDICTINE CADETS
WHO BRAVELY SACRIFICED
THEIR LIVES FOR OUR
NATION
IN WORLD WAR II

"GREATER LOVE THAN THIS NO MAN HATH THAT
A MAN LAY DOWN HIS LIFE FOR HIS FRIENDS"

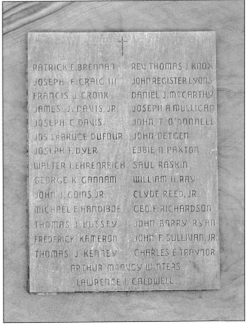

PATRICK E. BRENNAN REV. THOMAS J. KNOX
JOSEPH F. CRAIG III JOHN REGISTER LYONS
FRANCIS J. CRONK DANIEL J. McCARTHY
JAMES J. DAVIS, JR. JOSEPH A. MULLIGAN
JOSEPH C. DAVIS JOHN T. O'DONNELL
JOS. LABRUCE DUFOUR JOHN OETGEN
JOSEPH F. DYER EBBIE N. PAXTON
WALTER I. EHRENREICH SAUL RASKIN
GEORGE K. GANNAM WILLIAM H. RAY
JOHN J. GOINS, JR CLYDE REED, JR.
MICHAEL F. HANDIBOE GEO. F. RICHARDSON
THOMAS J. HUSSEY JOHN BARRY RYAN
FREDERICK KAMERON JOHN F. SULLIVAN, JR.
THOMAS J. KENNEY CHARLES E. TRAYNOR
ARTHUR McAVOY WINTERS
LAWRENCE L. CALDWELL

GANNAM DAY AT BENEDICTINE. At left, three cadets on flag detail pose next to the war memorial. With the war memorial completed, the Gannam Day ceremonies were eventually moved to the Benedictine campus (below) where the traditions begun at the Gannam home have been observed every Pearl Harbor Remembrance Day since then. The George K. Gannam American Legion Post No. 184 has been part of the ceremony ever since its participation in the flagpole ceremony in 1945, helping to plan the event as well as providing a wreath to lay at the foot of the memorial. The tradition of giving the flag used in the day's ceremony to the Gannam family was begun at this time; today, the family gives the flag back to the school for use throughout the year.

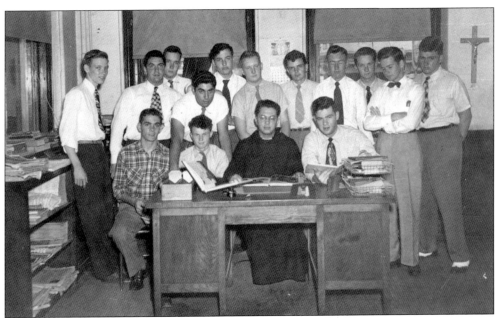

STAFF OF *THE BENEDICTINE CADET*, C. **1946.** Pictured is the staff of the school newsletter, with Fr. Bede Lightner, the recently assigned principal of Benedictine Military School, in 1946. The name of the newsletter was changed from *The Campus Quill* to *The Benedictine Cadet* during the mid-1940s. It was published seven times a year and included as part of its masthead the slogan "For God, Country, and Benedictine."

FORSYTH PARK EXTENSION, C. **1950.** A company of cadets poses in Forsyth Park at order arms. With the addition of the armory/gymnasium at the back of the campus drill field and the steady growth of the student population, the Benedictine Corps of Cadets began to march to Forsyth Park Extension, which was originally intended for military reviews, for drill practice and military exercises during the 1940s and 1950s.

COMMISSIONING DANCE. At left, a cadet and his date pose in front of the floral arch around 1947. During the 1940s and 1950s, Benedictine held four dances a year: commissioning, Christmas, St. Patrick's Day, and for the upperclassmen, the junior-senior prom. Commissioning and the other dances were generally held in the armory/gymnasium (below) while the prom was held at the city auditorium on the corner of Bull and East Anderson Streets.

BENEDICTINE DRILL TEAM, C. 1946.
The Benedictine drill team are on
the field during halftime of the 1946
Thanksgiving Day football game between
Benedictine and Savannah High School
(below). According to Maurice Sheppard
in his book *Savannah's Thanksgiving
Day Football Classic*, "Benedictine's
contribution [to the halftime shows] was
their marching band and an excellent
demonstration by their prize drill
team. . . . The demonstrations were silent
order drills with each cadet marching
precise drill routes in formation without
verbal commands. The prize drill team
would perform every year, and it was
always a thrill to witness their fine
performances."

GOLDEN JUBILEE CELEBRATION, C. 1952. Abbot Vincent Taylor, OSB, of Belmont Abbey (center above), monks of Sacred Heart Priory, and guest clergy pose on the porch of the priory while an honor guard of Benedictine Cadets stand at attention. This photograph was taken before the clergy processed to the church to celebrate a solemn pontifical Mass during a week of commemorative events marking the 50th anniversary of the founding of the school. In addition to two solemn pontifical Masses, events planned during the Golden Jubilee Week included a buffet supper for the clergy at the priory, an alumni banquet at the Desoto Hilton, and commencement exercises for the seniors at the city auditorium (below). The week of events culminated in a beach party for the clergy at Tybee Island.

JOHN E. "VIC" MELL, CLASS OF 1940. Coach Vic Mell is with, from left to right, players Henry Rape, Luke Sims, and Tom Brennan around 1961. Mell was head football and basketball coach at Benedictine from 1950 to 1968. During this time, he had a 60-percent winning record as a football coach, won 10 city championships and 2 region titles, and was awarded Region 2-AAA Coach of the Year in both football and basketball.

SACRED HEART CHURCH

Benedictine Fathers

Bull at 33rd Street

Savannah, Georgia

✝

MASSES

Sundays: 6:00, 7:00, 8:00, 9:00, 10:30, 12:15

Holy Days: 6:00, 7:00, 8:00, 9:00, 10:00, 12:15

Weekdays: 6:30, 7:00, 7:30

First Fridays: 6:30, 7:00, 7:30, 8:30 a.m. and 6:30 p.m.

DEVOTIONS

Rosary, Litany and Benediction: Sunday 6:15 p.m.

Sacred Heart Devotions: Fridays 6:15 p.m.

Holy Hour—First Fridays: 6:15 to 7:15 p.m.

CONFESSIONS

Weekdays: Before Masses

Saturdays and Vigils: 4:30 to 6:00 p.m. and 7:30 to 9:00 p.m.

✝

STANLEY IMPRESSIONS INC. N Y C

RED FISH & DAYS OF LENT - MAY EAT MEAT ONCE
BROWN FISH - DAYS OF ABSTINENCE

SACRED HEART CHURCH POCKET CALENDAR, C. 1955. These business card–sized pocket calendars were printed for parishioners of Sacred Heart Church to help them remember when to abstain from eating meat. The opposite side of the card indicates the days and times of Mass, devotions, and confessions. With 12 priest-monks in residence, the Benedictines of Sacred Heart Priory were able to efficiently allocate pastoral responsibilities among themselves in addition to their chaplain and teaching duties.

JAMES J. "JJ" FLYNN, CLASS OF 1959. Pictured is a family photograph of Benedictine Cadet Jimmy Flynn and his younger sister Betty Ann, a student at St. Vincent's Academy, posing in their respective school uniforms in front of their home around 1957. Since their founding in 1902 and 1845, respectively, Benedictine and St. Vincent's Academy, an all girls' school operated by the Sisters of Mercy, have always been the only Catholic high schools in Savannah and, therefore, a natural fit for Catholic families with sons and daughters.

FR. BEDE LIGHTNER, OSB, C. 1960. This portrait of Fr. Bede Lightner was taken to commemorate his silver jubilee as a monk. Father Bede was ordained a priest in 1941 and was first assigned to Belmont High School and College where he was rector from 1942 to 1946. He taught at the other BC (Benedictine High School) in Richmond, Virginia, in 1945–1946. He served as principal of Benedictine Military School from 1946 until being named prior of the Benedictine community in Savannah in 1960.

BENEDICTINE CHEERLEADERS, C. 1960. Posed in Lafayette Square are Benedictine cheerleaders, from left to right, Mary Woodward, Patty Brennan, Sandra Chan, Sherry O'Neil, Betty Ann Flynn (captain), Margie Dobson, Bobby Finnigan, Mary Kavanaugh, and Barbara McBride. After 1950, students of St. Vincent Academy, Benedictine's sister school, made up the cheerleading squad for the Benedictine football team, a tradition that continues to the present. (Courtesy of Betty Ann Ciucevich.)

FOUNDERS OF THE INDEPENDENT SACRED HEART PRIORY OF SAVANNAH, C. 1961. In 1961, Sacred Heart Priory was granted independence from Belmont Abbey. This photograph was included in an article in the *Savannah Morning News-Press* announcing the new arrangement and identifying the founding members of the monastic community, from left to right, (seated) Frs. Norbert McGowan, Bede Lightner, Denis Strittmatter, and Stephen Dowd; (standing) Frs. Aloysius Wachter, Terrance Kernan, Christopher Johann, Peter Trizzino, Luke Bain, Timothy Flaherty, Andrew Doris, and Damian Muldowney.

THE PROBLEM

The problem itself is quite simple — growth. In the last twenty-five years the student enrollment at Benedictine has more than doubled (as shown graphic-ally in the chart below). Moreover, in the last ten years alone, students have increased from two hundred and two to three hundred and thirty-five.

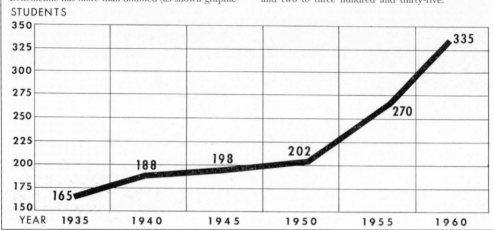

STUDENTS

188 · 198 · 202 · 270 · 335 · 165

YEAR: 1935 · 1940 · 1945 · 1950 · 1955 · 1960

GROWING PAINS, 1950s. The chart above illustrates the dramatic growth the school experienced over the decades. With enrollment skyrocketing and the old college building, only constructed to accommodate 200 students, no longer suiting the needs of the school and monastic community, the monks began to plan for a new campus on Savannah's suburban south side, purchasing a wooded 111-acre tract in 1958, the same year that the priory received a bequest of $500,000. The land was originally part of the Brown Farm, the county prison work farm (below). The semi-remote, wooded site was ideal for a monastery as the Chatham County Board of Commissioners had reserved the surrounding land for the establishment of local administrative offices and other government departments.

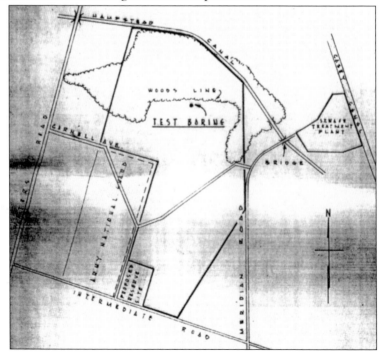

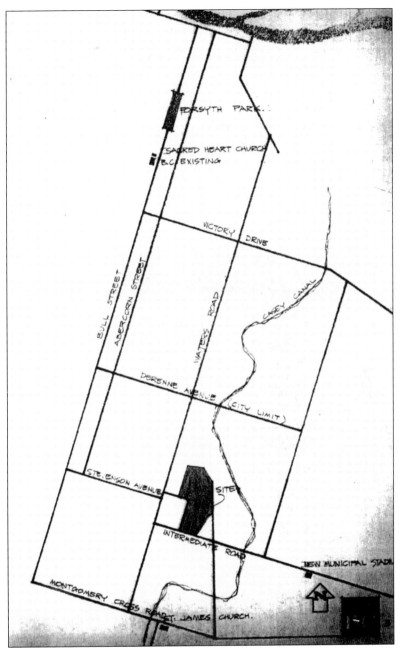

LOCATION MAP OF NEW CAMPUS SITE, C. 1958. This map prepared by Thomas and Hutton shows the existing Bull Street campus and the new 111-acre site on Intermediate Road (later renamed Eisenhower Drive). St. James Church, established by the Benedictines as a mission of Sacred Heart Parish in 1949, and Memorial Stadium are both depicted. As part of their sustainability plan for the new campus (and continued ascension to abbatial status), it is likely that the Benedictines had hoped to cede Sacred Heart to the diocese in return for parochial duties at St. James. The close proximity of Memorial Stadium was a key selling point used in the Benedictines' development campaign; the stadium has traditionally been considered the unofficial home field of the Benedictine football team since its completion in 1961.

97

COMMISSIONING, C. 1959. The members of the faculty and honored guests are processing down the middle of the armory, led by the color guard as the Corps of Cadets, assembled on each side, stands at present arms. By the late 1950s, the Corps of Cadets had grown to four companies, rendering the original armory barely serviceable to accommodate such functions as commissioning and other events.

Seven

BUILDING THE NEW SEAWRIGHT DRIVE CAMPUS

We monks of Sacred Heart Priory have tried to build for the future. We pray that within these walls will be found the spirit of St. Benedict. . . . It is here that must be fulfilled the faith that has inspired a mere handful of religious to identify themselves for life with this city of Savannah.

—Fr. Bede Lightner, OSB

Facing similar needs for expansion, many Benedictine communities in the United States launched extensive building programs during this time, commissioning well-known architects to design master plans to guide the growth of their abbeys and associated schools, culminating in a watershed of groundbreaking Modernist architecture. Rather than imitate the traditional styles of the past, such as Romanesque or Gothic, the monks opted for modern architecture because they wanted to adopt an architecture that was new and of this time, an architecture that would better reflect the contemporary culture and postwar, technology-driven society in which they now lived. Between 1958 and 1963, Benedictine communities at St. John's Abbey in Collegeville, Minnesota; St. Gregory's Abbey in Portsmouth, Rhode Island; Annunciation Priory in Bismark, North Dakota; St. Louis Abbey in Missouri; and others, commissioned Modernist architects to design ambitious, innovative, and site-specific new architecture for their monasteries and schools. Duncan Stroik, a noted ecclesiastical architect and editor of the journal *Sacred Architecture*, refers to this period of innovation in "The Roots of Modernist Church Architecture," writing that the "Benedictines in the U.S. were the equivalent of the Dominicans in France, being great patrons of Modernist art and architecture, as well as being liturgically progressive" and describes the buildings constructed during this period as "sleek, nontraditional and critically acclaimed by the architectural establishment."

Savannah's Benedictine campus and priory was planned and developed during this same period, roughly between 1958 and 1964, and was part of this national trend that was occurring within the Benedictine monastic community in the United States. Having been granted independence from Belmont Abbey in 1961, the monks of Sacred Heart Priory had accepted Savannah as their home for life and set about planning the new school campus and monastery—their new site of stability and their spiritual home.

A 35-year master plan for the campus was designed by the Savannah firm of Thomas, Driscoll, and Hutton that called for two phases of construction: an initial phase consisting of an academic building, cafeteria, armory-gymnasium, small chapel, and monastery, and a second phase consisting of dormitories and a larger church to be built at a later time.

THE BENEDICTINE CADET

Vol. IV, No. 4   Benedictine Military School, Savannah, Ga.   February 16, 1961

BENEDICTINE BEGINS EXPANSION PROGRAM

PLANNED FOR IMMEDIATE CONSTRUCTION ARE:
1. Main (Anderson Memorial) Building. 2. Gymnasium- Armory, Cafeteria. 3. Faculty Residence. 4. Chapel. 5.Football Field. 6. Baseball Field. 7. Parking Area.

Campaign Is Key Point

For the first time in its 59-year history Benedictine is appealing to parents of students, alumni, and friends in the community for financial help with building efforts. This appeal is the key point of a $1,250,000 building program launched on February 1. Hopes have been expressed that the building program on a recently purchased tract on Intermediate Road will be underway by January 1962.

Executive committee members of the Benedictine Development Campaign are Gen. Richard H. Mayer, credit manager of the Chatham Furniture Co., Andrew J. Ryan, Jr., solicitor general of the Eastern Judicial Circuit of Georgia; Bernie Slotin, a director of Slotin and Co. and a member of the Chatham County Board of Education, and Father Bede, principal of Benedictine.

The present building program will relieve a critical space shortage now existing at Benedictine and will take care of anticipated growth for the next five to seven years.

New buildings planned for immediate construction are as follows:

—A main (Anderson Memorial) building, containing administrative offices, a library, a cafeteria, 14 classrooms, three science laboratories, and a commercial room. This will be so constructed that it can be expanded.

—Outdoor sports facilities consisting of a football field, track, and baseball diamond.

—A gymnasium-armory (seating capacity 2,000) containing a basketball court, two classrooms, two offices, two locker rooms, two show rooms, athletic storage facilities, a rifle room, and a band practice room.

B.C. to Host   NEWS BRIEFS   Patterson Named

THE BENEDICTINE CADET, c. FEBRUARY 1961. A 35-year master plan for the new campus and priory was designed by the Savannah architectural and engineering firm Thomas, Driscoll, and Hutton that called for two phases of construction. The new academic campus was specifically designed for a military school and would have ample room for a drill field as well as facilities for boarding students, a sign that the monks planned to expand the military aspect of the school even further. In addition, the monastery was planned to accommodate up to 20 monks as the newly independent monastic community aspired to rise to the rank of abbey within the next several years.

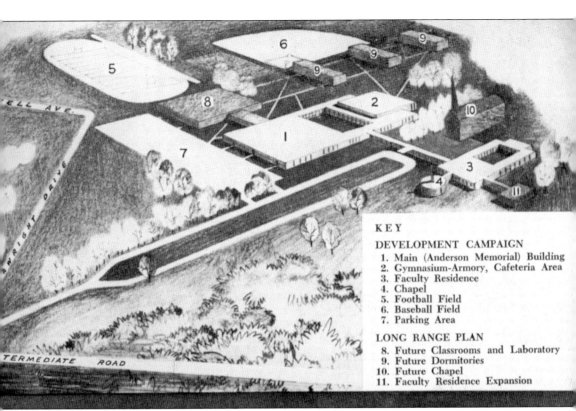

KEY

DEVELOPMENT CAMPAIGN
1. Main (Anderson Memorial) Building
2. Gymnasium-Armory, Cafeteria Area
3. Faculty Residence
4. Chapel
5. Football Field
6. Baseball Field
7. Parking Area

LONG RANGE PLAN
8. Future Classrooms and Laboratory
9. Future Dormitories
10. Future Chapel
11. Faculty Residence Expansion

PROPOSED SITE PLAN, C. 1961. Although this plan had changed considerably by the time ground was broken in 1963, several aspects remained the same, such as the design for the monastery and chapel. Two elements of the long-range plan—construction of a parish church (No. 10) and dormitories for boarding students (No. 9)—were key components of the sustainability plan developed by the newly established conventual priory. News articles written after the completion of the first phase of construction indicate that a $175,000 church, swimming pool, tennis courts, 17 additional classrooms, and a 100-double-bedroom dormitory were all planned for the future. The estimated cost to complete both phases was set at $2,325,000, a very large sum for 1963.

AERIAL VIEW OF SEAWRIGHT DRIVE CAMPUS, C. 1965. This aerial photograph of the new campus was taken shortly after its completion. Clockwise from top left are the cafetorium, armory-gymnasium, academic building, monastery, and chapel. The buildings and layout of the new Benedictine campus were designed by an innovative young architect, Juan Carlos Bertotto, who was schooled in the Bauhaus tradition while attending Georgia Tech's School of Architecture,

from which he graduated in 1958. In planning the Benedictine campus, Bertotto clearly drew inspiration from the landmark works of the Modernist architects he studied while he was a student at Georgia Tech—Frank Lloyd Wright ("esplanades" or concrete canopies); Mies van der Rhoe (cafetorium); Marcel Breuer (concrete canopies/campus layout), and most especially, Eero Saarinen (chapel and armory-gymnasium).

103

ST. JOHN'S ABBEY CHURCH, C. 1955. This photograph of St. John's Abbey Church was taken around 1955. The Savannah Benedictines and their confreres at other Benedictine communities in the United States chose modern architecture not out of a preference for an architectural style but through a shared belief that Modernism could best translate their Benedictine ideals into a built form that would also satisfy their responsibility, as prescribed in the Rule of St. Benedict, to "share in the creation of a new future," a sentiment best expressed in 1953 by Abbot Baldwin of St. John's Abbey:

> The Benedictine tradition at its best challenges us to think boldly and to cast
> our ideals in forms which will be valid for centuries to come, shaping them with
> all the genius of present-day materials and techniques. We feel that the modern
> architect with his orientation toward functionalism and honest use of materials
> is uniquely qualified to produce a Catholic work. In our position it would, we
> think, be deplorable to build anything less, particularly since our age and our
> country have thus far produced so little truly significant religious architecture.

(Courtesy of the Historic American Buildings Survey, Library of Congress, Prints and Photographs Division).

CHAPEL AND MONASTERY. Bertotto and the Thomas, Driscoll, and Hutton team designed most of the buildings on the campus in the New Formalist style of modern architecture that was in vogue at the time, an architecture that incorporated the building forms of the past but expressed them in Modernist terms using contemporary materials and technology. Bertotto employed historic precedent in his design for the campus as a way of alluding to the Benedictine Order's medieval monastic heritage through its association with the Gothic style. The Benedictines have always been great patrons of the arts and architecture, having been among the first to embrace the Gothic style at Saint-Denis Abbey during the 12th century and among the first to embrace Modernism in the 20th century. This symbolic use of the Gothic style is no more apparent than in Bertotto's design for the priory chapel (above) and monastery (below).

KRESGE CHAPEL, MASSACHUSETTS INSTITUTE OF TECHNOLOGY (MIT), C. 1955. The priory chapel (below) is a clever reinterpretation of Eero Saarinen's iconic Kresge Chapel (left), completed in 1955 at MIT in Cambridge, Massachusetts. In adapting Saarinen's design, Bertotto appropriated the scale, form, and basic materials of the Kresge Chapel, as well as the reflecting pool, or "moat," while adding intervals of thin vertical windows embellished with austere Gothic buttressing and ornament. He also retained the enclosed walkway that Saarinen used to connect his chapel to a small office and library, although utilized here to connect the chapel to the monastery. (Left, courtesy of the Balthazar Korab collection of photographs showing Eero Saarinen architecture, Library of Congress, Prints and Photographs Division.)

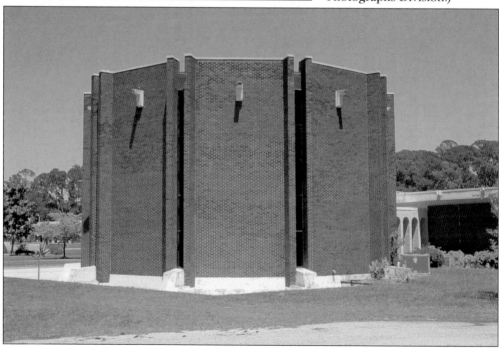

PRIORY CHAPEL, C. 1965. A promotional photograph of the chapel was taken at night (above). Bertotto was likely drawn to Saarinen's modern circular chapels based on his understanding of medieval monastic precedent, and since the priory chapel was originally designed for use as a chapter house, he appropriated the form of the 13th-century English chapter house since they too were characteristically free standing, mostly polygonal yet sometimes circular, and were attached to the side of an associated cathedral by a hyphen-like vestibule.

MONASTERY. Bertotto also based the design of his contemporary monastery on historical precedent while expressing it in modernistic terms. The monastery conveys Gothic inspiration through its round-headed, cantilevered windows; thin cast-concrete water spouts jutting through the roof parapets; and heavy batten wood doors. The monastery's floor plan resembles a 12th-century Carthusian charter house as the monk's cells open directly into the cloister walk, which is enclosed by glass on the exterior.

ARMORY-GYMNASIUM, C. 1965. This photograph of the daily muster of the Corps of Cadets on the plaza in front of the armory-gymnasium was taken during the 1964–1965 school year. The armory-gymnasium is the signature building of the academic campus and was designed to represent the military heritage of the school, serving both as a memorial and as a multiuse facility for sports and military, religious, and school ceremonies and functions. The concrete pavilion in front of the building was meant to serve as a focal point for daily military exercises as well as solemn religious ceremonies. Pictured below is a c. 1964 dedication ceremony. The flagpole is in the center of the pavilion, perfectly aligned with the memorial plaques embedded in the building's façade; its location is intended to honor the 30 Benedictine Cadets who died during World War II and to provide the Corps of Cadets with a daily reminder of their sacrifice.

CONCRETE CANOPIES. The above aerial photograph of the campus was taken in the 1970s, and the c. 1987 photograph below is of the Corps of Cadets assembled on the plaza in front of the academic building. The preform, reinforced concrete canopies that connect all of the buildings on the campus were inspired in part by the modern concrete covered walkways designed by internationally renowned architect Marcel Breuer during the 1950s for St. John's Abbey in Collegeville, Minnesota, as well as the monastery and college campus he designed for the Benedictine Sisters of Annunciation Priory, North Dakota, during the early 1960s. The cantilevered superstructure of the armory-gymnasium serves as a continuation of the concrete canopies that flank both sides of the academic quad and monastic green.

ESPLANADES, FLORIDA SOUTHERN COLLEGE. The idea to use independent covered walkways in a campus setting was not new, as Frank Lloyd Wright famously used esplanades (above) to "create a sense of continuity of design" throughout the Lakeland campus he designed for Florida Southern College between 1941 and 1958. Bertotto's concrete covered walkways at Benedictine (below) share many similarities with Wright's esplanades. They are a major component of the campus design; they are freestanding and extend along the length of buildings; concrete block retaining walls often form the inner walls of the walkways and double as planters when extending along buildings; and they are stepped at building entrances. (Above, courtesy of the Historic American Buildings Survey collection of photographs showing Frank Lloyd Wright architecture, Library of Congress, Prints and Photographs Division.)

CAFETORIUM, C. 1963. The photograph above of the cafetorium, which was half cafeteria and half auditorium/assembly space, was taken in 1963 as the building neared completion. Note the completed concrete canopies and plaza in front of the building. The International-style cafetorium is the only building on campus that is not an example of New Formalism; it was likely designed by principal architect Porter Driscoll, a proponent of Mies van der Rohe. At Benedictine, the geometry of the cloister is everywhere, from the subtle symbolism of the sunken courts that form the heart of the plans for the cafetorium (below) and the academic building, where Mass was originally celebrated for the student population, to the monastic origins of the campus's traditional collegiate quadrangle plan.

Merry Times
Est. 1899
August, 1964
BRICK GOES TO MILITARY SCHOOL
JUMBOS BUILD THE BIG ONES
WELL-KNOWN FIRMS USE MERRY BRICK

***MERRY TIMES* NEWSLETTER, C. 1964.** Benedictine's new Modernist campus was well received and garnered coverage in all of the local and several regional newspapers, including a nice article in the *Atlanta-Journal Constitution*, "Modern Beauty for Old Savannah," in which the reporter describes the campus as "both modern and medieval," and as "Camelot revived in the piney woods of the old Brown Farm," and describes the chapel interior (below) as a "castle-like . . . room waiting for King Arthur and his knights." Merry Brothers Brick and Tile Company of Augusta, Georgia, the largest manufacturer of its kind in the country at the time, featured the BC Campus in its monthly promotional newsletter (left), which praised the inspired work of architect Juan Carlos Bertotto: "The excellence of design and unusual architectural treatment, unifying a complex assortment of buildings into a harmonious grouping, have drawn wide attention from both professional and lay sources."

REVEILLE, FIRST DAY OF CLASSES AT SEAWRIGHT DRIVE CAMPUS, C. 1963. Corps of Cadets are in formation on the plaza on the first day of classes at the new Seawright Drive campus (above). The first day of classes at Benedictine's new campus was September 23, 1963. Although construction crews worked overtime to complete the campus by the beginning of the school year, only the academic building, cafetorium, plaza, and concrete canopies were completed by this time. Among the young men who reported to campus that day was the school's first African American student, making Benedictine one of the first schools in Savannah to begin to integrate. The chapel (seen under construction below), monastery, and armory-gymnasium were completed by early 1964. (Both, courtesy of the Diocese of Savannah Archives & Records Management Office.)

DEDICATION OF SACRED HEART PRIORY AND BENEDICTINE MILITARY SCHOOL. Savannah bishop Thomas J. McDonough and clergy are on the concrete podium in front of the armory-gymnasium during the benediction of the most blessed sacrament. According to the 1965 *Sabre* yearbook, "April 30, 1964 was a milestone in the history of the Benedictine Order in Savannah. On that date, on a clear spring sky, the complex of buildings that comprises Benedictine Military School was formally and solemnly dedicated. It was a day that will live in the memories of all of us for the rest of our lives." Bishop Walters of the Diocese of Raleigh, Bishop Francis Reh of Charleston, and Abbot Walter Coggin of Belmont Abbey were among the many dignitaries present. (Above, courtesy of Belmont Abbey; below, courtesy of the Diocese of Savannah Archives & Records Management Office.)

DEDICATION CEREMONY AND BLESSING OF BUILDINGS. As seen through the concrete canopies, guests and clergy are seated on the plaza in front of the concrete podium pavilion of the armory-gymnasium during the dedication ceremonies at Benedictine. Preceding the benediction, Bishop Thomas J. McDonough of Savannah and a procession of clergy moved through and blessed each of the buildings on campus. The photograph below is of Bishop McDonough (center), assisted by Fr. Christopher Johann, OSB, principal of Benedictine (at left), and Fr. Terrance Kernan, OSB, pastor of Sacred Heart Church (to the right of Bishop McDonough), blessing the lobby of the academic building. (Above, courtesy of Belmont Abbey; below, courtesy of the Diocese of Savannah Archives & Records Management Office.)

PRIORY SCENES, C. 1965. Here are promotional photographs of the priory and chapel taken shortly after their completion. Between 1962 and 1964, Sacred Heart Priory mourned the deaths of three monks. The loss of three monk-teachers put a strain on the school's manpower, making it necessary to hire lay teachers. The added expense of the teacher's salaries, in addition to a sharp decline in enrollment, put a strain on the priory's finances and made it increasingly difficult for the Benedictine community to satisfy its financial obligations. With the school operating at a deficit and bills mounting, the future of the nascent independent priory and of Benedictine Military School looked bleak. This sentiment is best expressed in the 1965 *Sabre* on a page captioned "Priory Scenes," which features various photographs of the priory and included this prescient phrase at the bottom of the page: "To be or not to be."

Eight

BENEDICTINE PRIORY

Forward, always forward, everywhere forward! We must not be held back by debts, bad years, or by difficulties of the times. Man's adversity is God's opportunity.

—Archabbot Boniface Wimmer, OSB

In 1967, the bishop of Savannah and the president of the American-Cassinese Congregation of Benedictine Monasteries put in motion the necessary canonical proceedings for the suppression of Sacred Heart Priory. The death of three founding members of the community as well as a sharp decrease in enrollment (from 335 students to 285 in 1963, a 15-percent decrease) eventually put the priory and school in a significant amount of debt, forcing the monks to seek the assistance of fellow congregation members. Finding that Sacred Heart Priory "did not have the strength of manpower and resources to exist any longer as an independent priory," the community was dissolved.

Benedictines from St. Vincent Archabbey in Latrobe assumed responsibility of the school and monastery, renamed Benedictine Priory, in the summer of 1967, making any changes deemed necessary to make the school economically viable and to pay down the debt incurred as a result of the building campaign. The most immediate and visible changes the St. Vincent monks made when the school reopened for the 1967–1968 school year was the termination of the compulsory four-year, full-military program; the creation of new non-military uniforms; and the changing of the name of the school to Benedictine High School (as the emphasis on the military aspects of the school had been dramatically toned down). Under pressure from alumni, a compulsory two-year military program was implemented the following year, and the name of the school was changed back to Benedictine Military School. Under the guidance of Fr. Aelred Beck, OSB, Benedictine's new headmaster, school enrollment increased substantially, and the debt was eventually retired. In 1972, Benedictine Priory awarded the Benedictine Medal of Excellence—its highest honor—to Fr. Bede Lightner, OSB, former principal and prior of Sacred Heart Priory, for his "thirty years of dedicated service to youth, particularly at BC" and for his leadership in bringing to fruition Benedictine's modern, state-of-the-art campus, "considered one of the finest high school plants in the South." By the time of Father Bede's return to the campus he helped plan and build, student enrollment at Benedictine had risen to 480, the highest it had ever been in its 70-year history.

MONASTIC COMMUNITY OF BENEDICTINE PRIORY, SAVANNAH, C. 1975. The Benedictine community pose on the steps of the academic court in the center of the academic building (above). Pictured are, from left to right, (first row) Frs. Blaine Resko, Bede Hasso, Ralph Bailey, Arthur Holtz, Aelred Beck, Anthony Wesolowski, and Albert Bickerstaff; (second row) Frs. Bertrand Dunegan, Bristan Takacj, and Wilfred Dumm; Br. Gerard Klaric; Fr. Briant Halloran; Br. Bernard Lewitzke; and Fr. Philip Ghys. Several of these monks were among the original group who came from St. Vincent Archabbey to assume responsibility of the school and priory in 1967. Fathers Bertrand, Wilfred, Anthony, and Albert, Brother Gerard, and Father Philip spent most of their monastic lives in service to Benedictine Military School. The photograph of the community below was taken in 1974.

SACRED HEART SCHOOL GRADUATION, C. 1968. Fr. Timothy Flaherty and Fr. Terrance Kernan pose with the graduating class of Sacred Heart Grammar School. Following the suppression of Sacred Heart Priory in 1967, the monks were given the opportunity to join another Benedictine community or to secularize (leave the order). While several chose to affiliate with other Benedictine communities, Fathers Kernan and Timothy chose to remain at Sacred Heart Church as priests of the Diocese of Savannah.

FR. AELRED BECK, OSB, HEADMASTER OF BENEDICTINE, 1967–1977. Father Aelred receives a check for the annual Fenian Society Scholarship in 1975. Father Aelred served as prior of the monastery and headmaster of Benedictine from 1967 to 1977. He guided Benedictine through a difficult transition in which many necessary changes were made that proved instrumental to the continued viability of the school. During Father Aelred's tenure, the size of the student body nearly doubled. (Courtesy of the Diocese of Savannah Archives & Records Management Office.)

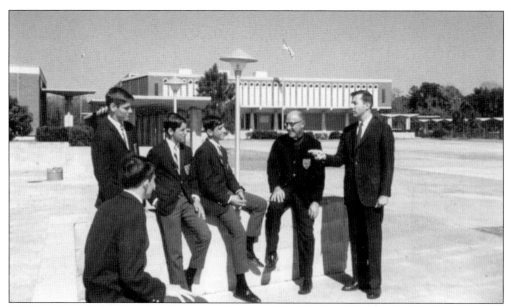

NON-MILITARY UNIFORMS, C. 1968. Talking to several Benedictine students wearing their newly issued school uniforms are, from right to left, Fred S. Clark, a member of the class of 1954 and the first president of the Benedictine Alumni Association, and Father Aelred. Before 1968, Benedictine had a full-military program, and therefore, a military uniform was worn at all times. In addition to the maroon blazer, white dress shirt, striped tie, and grey slacks, cadets would now wear the standard-issued Army-green uniform on JROTC days.

SEN. ROY L. ALLEN II, CLASS OF 1968. Cadet Roy Allen, pictured in front on the right, marched with the Benedictine Drill Team in the St. Patrick's Day Parade in 1967. Allen was the first African American to graduate from Benedictine, rising to the rank of cadet major. He went on to become a successful lawyer and politician, serving as a county commissioner, state representative, and state senator before retiring from politics in 1994. (Courtesy of the City of Savannah Municipal Archives)

KEN "THE HAWK" HARRELSON. Ken Harrelson (class of 1959) poses with Father Aelred (left) and coach Vic Mell (center) around 1968. Between 1963 and 1971, Harrelson was an all-star first baseman and outfielder, finding his greatest success with the Boston Red Socks (1967–1969). He is best known for his 33-year tenure as a broadcast announcer for the Chicago White Sox. (Courtesy of the Diocese of Savannah Archives & Records Management Office.)

FR. ALBERT C. BICKERSTAFF, OSB. Father Albert (left) is talking to Father Aelred outside a classroom in C-Wing around 1970. Father Albert served on the faculty of Benedictine Military School from 1967 to 1992, teaching religion and social studies as well as coaching basketball, football, and golf. In 1997, he returned to Benedictine as director of campus ministry, a position he held until his death from cancer in 2003. In 2020, Benedictine's new turf football field complex was named in his honor.

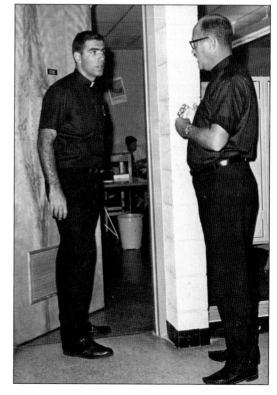

GRADUATION, CLASS OF 1969. The graduating class of 1969 poses in "the Well," the common name for the academic court, wearing their caps and gowns. Before 1968, all preceding graduating classes wore their dress military uniforms for graduation exercises. With the elimination of the full-military program, graduates wore caps and gowns over their new school uniforms for the first time in school history.

CENTENARY CELEBRATION, 1874–1974. A concelebrated Mass was held in the Benedictine gymnasium as part of the week's centenary celebration, commemorating 100 years of spiritual and educational service to the people of the South, according to the program. The principal concelebrants for the Mass were Bishop Raymond Lessard of Savannah, Archabbot Egbert Donovan of St. Vincent Abbey, Abbot Edmond McCafferty of Belmont Abbey, and Abbot Fidelis Dunlop of St. Leo Abbey, Florida.

FR. CONAN FEIGH, OSB, AND FR. MEINRAD LAWSON, OSB. Fathers Conan (left) and Meinrad concelebrate Mass in the cafetorium around 1980. Father Conan succeeded Father Aelred as prior and headmaster in 1977 and served in that capacity until 1987. Father Meinrad served at Benedictine from 1978 to 2001 as a member of the faculty and in the administration of the school and priory. His various roles included prior (1987–1999), headmaster (1994–1996), and first president of BC (1996–1999).

LIBRARY AND MEDIA CENTER, C. 1985. The media center is pictured under construction during the spring of 1985. The new media center wing provided much-needed additional space for the library as well as providing other educational opportunities, such as video production, computer graphics, daily school newscasts, and later, a computer lounge. The addition also featured a theater/performance space and Alumni Hall, a spacious corridor where the composite photograph of every graduating class of Benedictine Military School is displayed.

MONASTIC COMMUNITY OF BENEDICTINE PRIORY, C. 1985. The monks of Benedictine Priory concelebrating Mass for the student population around 1985 are, from right to left, Frs. Albert Bickerstaff, Bertrand Donegan, David Griffin, Ronald Gatman, Meinrad Lawson (center), Wilfred Dumm, and Philip Ghys; not pictured are Fr. Anthony Wesolowski and Br. Tim Brown. Brother Tim and Father Ronald are currently the longest-tenured members of Benedictine Priory, serving 39 years in the media center and 41 years in religious studies, respectively.

FR. WILFRED DUMM, OSB, C. 1985. Fr. David Griffin, OSB, (left), assistant headmaster of Benedictine; Fr. Wilfred Dumm, OSB, (center); and his brother Fr. Demetrius Dumm, OSB, pose in Alumni Hall on the 40th anniversary of Father Wilfred's ordination. Father Wilfred taught physics, math, and electronics at BC from 1967 to 1996. After his retirement, he served as director of alumni at BC as well as national chaplain (1986–2002) of the US Power Squadron, of which he was a local member.

DEDICATION OF THE STUDENT/ALUMNI ATHLETIC CENTER, NOVEMBER 1990. Chairman of the building committee Walter C. Corish Jr. (class of 1961) and Brian Filmore (president of the class of 1991) place the cornerstone into the new athletic center as Fr. David Griffin, OSB, headmaster of Benedictine (1987–1994), and William J. Kehoe (class of 1919) look on. The new building added much needed locker space, a new weight room, racquetball courts, and offices. Members of the building committee included longtime Benedictine teacher and basketball coach Tommy Cannon (1972–2009, class of 1965), and head football coach Jim Walsh (1970–1994). Below is a construction photograph of the athletic center taken in August 1990. (Both, courtesy of the Diocese of Savannah Archives & Records Management Office.)

COMMISSIONED OFFICERS, CLASS OF 2010. Pictured are the recently commissioned officers of the 2010 graduating class of Benedictine Military School. Each year, the brigade undergoes the JROTC Program of Accreditation Inspection to ensure that all cadets are educated on correct military procedures and knowledge. For 33 consecutive years, the BC Corps of Cadets has maintained its position as an Honor Unit of Distinction, signifying that the brigade is rated in the top 20 percent in the nation.

BROWN STEM WING, C. 2017–2018. The new STEM wing was completed in 2018 as part of the Forward Always Forward capital campaign. Under the leadership of Fr. Frank Ziemkiewicz, OSB, headmaster of Benedictine (2007 to present), BC embarked on a capital campaign to construct a new academic wing, renovate existing classrooms, and improve athletic facilities and the campus environment. With Phase I complete and Phase II underway, the campaign has been the most successful fundraising drive in school history, with over $14 million pledged.

BIBLIOGRAPHY

Baumstein, Paschal. *My Lord Belmont: A Biography of Leo Haid*. Belmont, NC: The Archives of Belmont Abbey, 1985.

Cobbers, Arnt. *Marcel Breuer 1902–1981*. Los Angeles, CA: Taschen, 2007.

Klacsmann, Karen T. "Christopher Murphy Jr. (1902–1973)." *New Georgia Encyclopedia*. 02 January 2020. Web. 12 May 2020.

McDonogh, Gary Wray. *Black and Catholic in Savannah, Georgia*. Knoxville, TN: The University of Tennessee Press, 1993.

Oetgen, Jerome. *An American Abbot: Boniface Wimmer, OSB, 1809–1887*. Washington, DC: The Catholic University of America Press, 1997.

———. "The Origins of the Benedictine Order in Georgia." *Georgia Historical Quarterly* Vol. 53, No.2 (June 1969), pp. 165–183.

One Faith One Family, The Diocese of Savannah 1850–2000. Syracuse, NY: Signature Publications, 2000.

Seasoltz, R. Kevin. *A Sense of the Sacred: Theological Foundations of Christian Architecture and Art*. New York, NY: The Continuum International Publishing Group Inc., 2005.

Sheppard, Maurice. *Savannah's Thanksgiving Day Football Classic: Benedictine vs. Savannah High*. Savannah, GA: Maurice Sheppard LLC, 2008.

Temko, Allan. *Eero Saarinen*. New York, NY: George Braziller Inc., 1962.

DISCOVER THOUSANDS OF LOCAL HISTORY BOOKS FEATURING MILLIONS OF VINTAGE IMAGES

Arcadia Publishing, the leading local history publisher in the United States, is committed to making history accessible and meaningful through publishing books that celebrate and preserve the heritage of America's people and places.

Find more books like this at
www.arcadiapublishing.com

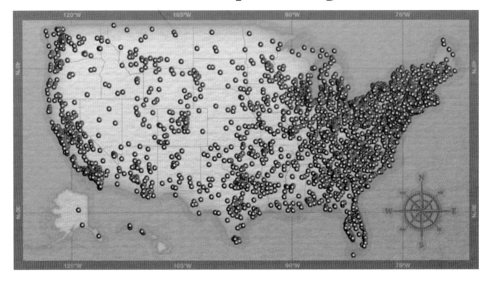

Search for your hometown history, your old stomping grounds, and even your favorite sports team.

Consistent with our mission to preserve history on a local level, this book was printed in South Carolina on American-made paper and manufactured entirely in the United States. Products carrying the accredited Forest Stewardship Council (FSC) label are printed on 100 percent FSC-certified paper.

MADE IN THE USA